Cowpokes to Bike Spokes

Other Titles by the Author

The Split Sky:
A Journey of Discovery in Utah's Nine Mile Canyon

White Canyon:
Remembering the Little Town at the Bottom of Lake Powell

To Be a Soldier

Cowpokes to Bike Spokes

The Story of Moab, Utah

TOM MCCOURT

Johnson Books
Boulder

Published by Johnson Books, a Big Earth Publishing company,
3005 Center Green Drive, Suite 220, Boulder, Colorado 80301.
E-mail: books@bigearthpublishing.com
www.bigearthpublishing.com
1–800–258–5830

Cover design by Jekaterina Girtakovska
Text design by Constance Bollen, cbgraphics

9   8   7   6   5   4   3   2   1

Library of Congress Cataloging-in-Publication Data
McCourt, Tom, 1946–
  The Moab story: cowpokes to bike spokes / Tom McCourt.
    p.   cm.
  ISBN-13: 978-1-55566-396-4
  1. Moab (Utah)—History. 2. Moab (Utah)—Description and travel. 3.
Moab (Utah)—
Biography. I. Title.
  F834.M6M35   2007
  979.2'58—dc22
                                    2007019302

Printed in Canada

To Marjorie Miller

Contents

Acknowledgments

A SPECIAL THANK YOU to Marjorie Miller, a Moabite woman who was the driving force behind this book. It was Marjorie who conceived and sold the idea for this book and then turned the project over to me, along with some valuable notes and source materials.

Thank you to others in the Moab area who have helped with this project, especially Eleanor Inskip of the Moab Museum and Sam Taylor of the *Times-Independent* newspaper.

Thanks also to Sue Ann Martel and the staff of the Western Railroad and Mining Museum of Helper, Utah. And to Jeff Bartlett and Karen Green of the College of Eastern Utah Prehistoric Museum in Price, Utah.

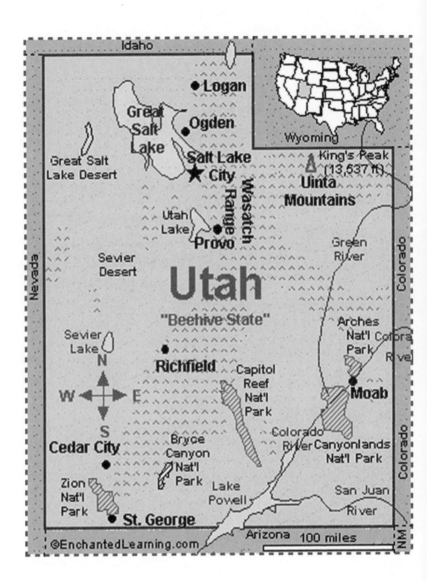

Idaho

Logan

Great Salt Lake

Ogden

Great Salt Lake Desert

Salt Lake City

Wyoming

King's Peak (13,537 ft)

Uinta Mountains

Wasatch Range

Nevada

Utah Lake

Provo

Sevier Desert

Green River

Colorado

Utah

"Beehive State"

Sevier Lake

N

Richfield

Capitol Reef Nat'l Park

Arches Nat'l Cotora Park

Rive

W

E

Moab

S

Colorado River

Canyonlands Nat'l Park

Cedar City

Bryce Canyon Nat'l Park

Lake Powell

San Juan

Zion Nat'l Park

St. George

River

Colorado

Arizona   100 miles

NM

x

Introduction

MY FIRST VISIT TO MOAB was in 1952. I went there with my grandparents, who were in the uranium business. It was love at first sight. And since that first visit when I was just a little boy, I have been able to visit often. I have lived my life in nearby Carbon County, only a few hours away. Over the years I have watched the town grow from a little farming community to the hub of Utah's mining industry to a world-class tourist destination, and I have marveled at the transition.

The town of Moab is a fascinating place with a fascinating history. But the reader should understand that this book is the "story" of Moab and not a "history" of the place. There is a difference. For one thing, storytelling is more fun. History tends to bog down in the minutia of events. When recounting history, too often the dates, names, facts, figures, and sources become all-important. Telling stories, on the other hand, still conveys the truth of historical events, but without the stress and clutter of academic anxiety.

And yet, all of the stories in this book are true and the necessary facts and figures are given. Scholars, historians, and people with enquiring minds can find volumes of supporting material if they choose to go there. The dusty facts and figures are available to anyone.

This book is intended to be light reading. It is written in the way I hope it will be enjoyed, like a good story around a campfire. And the complete story of Moab is too big to tell in a single book of this size, so I have sifted the material and collected only the gems that best outline the story in a brief and entertaining way.

Delicate Arch, Arches National Park
(author photo)

But when writing a condensed history, or story, like this, it is always the colorful and controversial characters who come to the spotlight: the Charlie Steens, Edward Abbeys, and Negro Bills of the world. Too often the real city fathers, the men and women who create the year-to-year story from behind the scenes, are hardly mentioned. People like the Taylor family (who has owned and managed the local newspaper since the days of cowboys and Indians), Ken McDougald, Tex McClatchy, George White, Justus Corbin, and dozens of others are given little or no space here. And yet many of those people deserve a biography all their own.

I have also skipped lightly over the most recent history of the town. The development of Moab's tourist industry is an interesting tale, but it too is a tangle of dates, names, places, and events better suited to scholarly recounting than casual reading. And besides, a person doesn't need to read about the modern town. Moab is there to be discovered and explored.

How Moab Got Its Name

 ames are important. We know people, places, and things by the names they are given. For good or bad, better or worse, a name is a tag that identifies, clarifies, and conveys useful information. Place names, especially, can be revealing. And so it is with a beautiful little town in southeastern Utah with the improbable name of Moab. The name is unique. No other town in America has that name, and the story behind it is as interesting as the name itself.

In 1879 the U.S. government established a mail route between Salina, Utah, and Ouray, Colorado. It was an ambitious undertaking. Eastern Utah was wild and unsettled in those days, and there were no good roads. The mail route was a 350-mile horse trail through the wilderness, and it was not the Pony Express. Mail was carried in panniers on the backs of packhorses or mules, and it sometimes took six weeks for a rider to complete the circuit and return. The route was infested with outlaws, wild Indians, and wild animals. The mail carrier packed a gun and a bedroll, camping at night along the trail.

The mail route followed parts of the Old Spanish Trail and crossed the Colorado River at the Old Spanish Crossing near present-day Moab. At that time there were a few hardy pioneers living in lower Spanish Valley, busy building cabins, tending cows, and planting gardens. The area was called by a variety of names: Little Grand Valley, Spanish Crossing, and Mormon Fort, among others. There was no town, only a collection of hardscrabble farms and ranches spread thin across the wilderness. The area was remote, and contact with the outside world was tenuous at best. To have a mail carrier pass through the area every month or two was like Neil Armstrong's radio link from the moon to planet earth.

Though few in number, residents of the area wanted a post office. To have a post office required an address. To have an address required a formal name. And so, the story goes, a committee of six was chosen from among the local pioneers to select an official name for the frontier outpost. The name they selected was "Moab." The Moab post office was opened in 1880, twenty-three years before the town was incorporated.

In later years, old pioneers said the name was suggested by William (Bill) Peirce, a local "scholar of the Bible." They also agreed that the name probably had some "religious significance." What that religious significance was is not spelled out in the literature. But an understanding of the Mormon background and mindset of the late 1800s offers some clues.

In the Bible, the land of Moab was beyond the River Jordan on the southeast side of the Dead Sea. It was a desert region on the very fringe of the Promised Land at the edge of the wilderness. The geographical location of Moab, Utah, in relation to the Great Salt Lake, combined with the wilderness setting, might have prompted that early group of pioneers to pick that name. Many of Moab's early settlers were Mormons, old Bill Peirce among them.

The Mormons saw many similarities between Utah and the Promised Land of the Bible. After all, they believed they had been led to Utah by a modern Moses named Brigham Young. Their wanderings in the wilderness had been on the great plains of the American West and not on the Sinai desert, but the similarities of the migration were close enough for the Latter-day Saints.

In the valleys of Utah the Mormons found their Promised Land, and the geography was amazingly similar to the land of Israel. There was the Great Salt Lake, very similar to the Dead Sea, and the salt lake was connected to Utah's Sea of Galilee (Utah Lake) by what the Mormons called the Jordan River—the River Jordan in biblical lingo. And far to the southeast of the lakes and settled valleys of northern Utah was a vast, uncharted wilderness of desert and sand. To the Mormons, it was the proper place to find the Land of Moab.

Mosquito Bite

There is another, less widely accepted possibility for the origin of the name. It has been suggested that the name "Moab" might actually be an Anglo corruption of a Paiute Indian name for the area. The Indian word "moapa" is said to mean "mosquito" or "mosquito water," and someone might have heard the natives use that term to describe the river bottom north of town.

Utah river bottoms have always grown some of the world's finest mosquitoes, and camping near the water must have been a backslapping experience in those early days before insecticides, mosquito netting, and bug repellants. The Indians generally avoided the "mosquito water" areas as a place to camp or live, preferring more elevated sites away from the river, where after-noon breezes fanned the heat and insects away.

It is easy to imagine a meeting between Paiutes and white men at a site chosen for a farm by an early group of settlers. A semi-naked Indian is watching in fascination as the settlers stack rocks and trim logs to build their home, swatting mosquitoes and mumbling obscenities as they toil. A great smudge pot of a fire is smoldering nearby and giving off copious amounts of smoke to try to discourage the bugs, but still they come in their millions.

A white man walks over, extends his hand in a gesture of good will, and says, "Howdy, Injun. Happy to have y'all as neighbors." Then, through signs, signals, and awkward charades, he asks the Indian, "What do you guys call this place?"

The Indian points at the fertile river bottom with its clouds of mosqui-toes and says, "Moapa," which means, by interpretation: "You silly white people are camping by the mosquito water. Ain't ya got no brains?"

"Moapa, eh," the white guy says. "You ignorant savages call this place Moapa?"

The white guy then turns to his sweating, mosquito-blistered friends and says, "Hey, guys, these here Injuns call this place Moapa. Too many vowels and syllables for me. I think we should anglicize the name to Moab. Whadya think?"

The Indian walks back to the hill where his friends and family are waiting in the cool, bug-free afternoon breeze. He stands for a while looking down on the mosquito-swatting homesteaders along the river bottom, and then he says in ancient Paiute, "Those newcomers are rich, but they sure are stupid."

A Town by Any Other Name . . .

From the beginning, some residents of Moab were unhappy about the name of the town. A controversy developed. People who were there at the time the name was selected were unable to confirm the exact intent behind it.

It could have been purely biblical, a way to link the town to other bible-like places in the Mormon Promised Land of Utah. But while the biblical Moab was the home of Ruth, one of the Bible's heroines, it is not the best of places in the biblical texts. The Moabites were sinners and worshippers of idols who often made war on God's chosen people. And worse than that, the biblical Moab was named after the bastard son of an incestuous relationship between Lott and his eldest daughter after their expulsion from Sodom and Gomorrah. The name "Moab" trampled on the proper Victorian sensibilities of the 1880s. What pious, God-fearing Christian would name a town Moab? Was old Bill Peirce making a tongue-in-cheek joke about the moral character of his pioneer neighbors? Probably not. But the whole thing might be interpreted that way. Some Moabites became rather sensitive about it. To them, the name was offensive.

As early as 1885, postmaster Henry Crouse tried unsuccessfully to have the name of the town changed to "Uvadalia." He might have been successful had he picked a name like Pleasant Valley,

Main Street in Moab, 1932
(Museum of Moab photo)

Cottonwood Glen, or even Spanish Valley—but Uvadalia? People smiled and decided to stick with Moab.

Five years later, in 1890, when Grand County was first incorporated and Moab designated the county seat, a petition went through the community suggesting a name change to "Vina." Grapes had recently been planted in the community and they showed real promise as a cash crop. And then, too, the petitioners felt that a proper county seat should have a name more fitting and dignified than "Moab," since the name was "unfavorably commemorative of an incestuous and idolatrous community existing 1897 years before the Christian era," according to *A History of Grand County* by Richard A. Firmage (Utah State Historical Society 1996). The new name should be "more appropriate, significant, or expressive of moral decency and manly dignity and in harmony with the progressive civilization of the present age." The petitioners thought "Vina" would be perfect.

Unfortunately—or fortunately, depending on your point of view—when the petition was presented to the County Court, there were only 59 signatures. The 1890 census showed 540 residents of the county. The court rejected the petition as not representing the wishes of the majority, and Moab has been Moab ever since.

The Magic Water of Matrimony Springs

Like magic, the cool, clean water splashes down from a pipe extending from a solid sandstone wall—a marvel to behold. The water is snowmelt that has traveled underground for twenty miles from the La Sal Mountains, passing through a natural filter of gravel and porous stone. The water is clear and uncontaminated—but it can also be deadly. There is a consequence for those who dare to drink. →

Matrimony Springs (author photo)

Legend says that in pioneer times, a young lady wishing to find a hus-band had only to get the young man of her choice to drink with her from the spring. The magic water would somehow bind them, and soon they would be married. Dances, parties, and picnics were often held on the riverbank near Matrimony Springs so young lovers could have easy access to Cupid's elixir. They say it worked every time.

In more recent years, it has been found that Matrimony Springs has another magic quality. People who drink from the spring are somehow drawn back to the Land of Moab again and again. The magic water binds them to the area.

So for those brave enough to tempt fate, Matrimony Springs can be found along the river road—Highway 128—about one-quarter-mile east of the Moab river bridge.

Moab Fever

In 1905 a traveler passing through Moab recorded his impressions. He was charmed with the town, the people, and the natural setting, and he made note of the slow pace of life in the little frontier community. In fact, he said the town physician told him that it was so easy to make a living and so hard to get rich in Moab that most of the townspeople suffered from a disease. The doctor called it Moab fever. He said the symptom was chronic laziness.

The statement was undoubtedly meant to be humorous. And there might even have been a grain of truth in the sentiment. But the good doctor was probably aware that there was another kind of Moab fever, a more potent strain that has infected hundreds over the years.

It is a selective disease and not everyone is infected. Poets and artists are most susceptible. While other people pass through the area and see only rocks, sage bushes, and dirt, poets partake of the magnificent scenery and the feeling of eternal wildness about the place. They get sand in their shoes, healing sunlight on their cheeks, joy in their heart, and peace in their soul. The desert rejuvenates them. Places like Moab are as vital to a poet's survival as water and air. And once a person has been infected with those emotional ties to the desert, Moab draws them back again, time after time.

Writer Edward Abbey had a bad case of Moab fever, but not any worse than some other people—he was only better able to communicate the symptoms. And like most of the rest of those afflicted, he didn't expect, or even want, to be cured.

But Moab fever goes back a long way. History and legend tell us that there's something about the Land of Moab that has drawn people there for centuries.

~~Anasazi~~ Ancestral Puebloans

* * *
☾ *

oday we know that there were several different Native American cultures in the Moab area over a period of many thousands of years. People didn't always understand that. To the early pioneers, there were only two groups of Indians: those they encountered in their daily travels, and those who had lived there in ancient times.

In pioneer days, there were Utes, Paiutes, and Navajos living near the settlements. Most homesteaders assumed they had always been there. But then they found evidence of another, older group of people, too—a mysterious culture long vanished. There were ruins and broken pottery in the canyons, and the evidence showed that the people of the ruins had lived lives much different from the historic tribes. They had been farmers, builders, and potters of the first order.

In the early 1800s, news began to spread of a "vanished race" of Indians who had lived in houses perched precariously like swallow nests on the sandstone walls of the canyon country. For want of a better name, this vanished race became known as the "cliff dwellers." The term "cliff dweller" prompts imagination, and many people who had never seen a cliff dwelling began to picture the cliff dwellers as a tribe of circus acrobats who spent their time on the ledges, performing feats of daring bravado like Stone Age trapeze artists. There was some speculation, too, that the cliff dwellers might have been rem-

An ancient Indian ruin in southern Utah (author photo)

nants of the lost tribes of Israel, shipwrecked Phoenicians, misplaced Aztecs, or even lost Egyptians who mummified their dead.

By the mid-1800s, the cliff dwellers had found another name and a more cohesive identity. They had become Moquis (spelled either Moki or Moqui), a Hopi word made popular by the early Spaniards. Moqui is interpreted to mean "old people"—or even "dead people"— and inexplicably, the Spaniards applied that name to the Hopi people in general. Father Escalante labeled the Hopi towns as "Moqui" settlements on his famous map of the Dominquez–Escalante expedition of 1776.

The name stuck, and to early settlers of the Utah frontier, any Pueblo Indian, living or dead, became a Moqui. The early Mormon missionary and explorer Jacob Hamblin visited the Moqui (Hopi) villages in the 1850s and wrote about it in his journals. Hamblin and his fellows also explored many of the "Moqui" ruins in Arizona and southern Utah.

Lacking professional guidance in archaeology and anthropology, but abounding in curiosity and imagination, the early pioneers made up the ancient Moqui as they went along. As they explored the caves and cliff dwellings, they made inferences from personal observations. To many, it was obvious that the ancient Moqui had been a race of midgets or dwarfs. Who else could have squeezed through those tiny doorways and lived in those impossibly small cliff houses? And the midget Moquis made itsy-bitsy little arrow points and grew very small, midget-sized ears of corn. They must have been a tribe of pygmies. The evidence was clear.

Through fantasy and imaginative storytelling, the mysti-cal Moqui came to be like the "little people" of Ireland or the Hobbits of modern fiction. Some imagined them to have lived like troops of monkeys in the high recesses of the cliffs. Such fanciful tales easily become rooted in folklore, and stories were told of the midget Moquis well into the twentieth century. Even today, some people in southern Utah still refer to cliff dwellings as "Moqui houses."

But then came Richard Weatherill, a controversial figure who unraveled the true cultural sequence of the four-corners area. Richard was a cowboy who discovered Mesa Verde and then became a self-taught archaeologist. Some have called him a pothunter, but he told us most of what we know today about the ancient cultures of the Southwest. All of the professional archaeologists since 1910 have made only fine-tuning adjustments and taxonomical observations, coloring within the lines of what Richard Weatherill sketched for us in the 1890s. Weatherill and his brothers debunked the Moqui myth. The cliff dwellers were not midgets, dwarfs, or Hobbits.

At the Pecos archaeological conference of 1927, the Moqui offi-cially became the Anasazi, a term Richard Weatherill had begun using in the 1890s. Anasazi is a Navajo word that has the proper meter and multi-syllabic structure to sound exotic and make it hard to pronounce by English speakers. It was the perfect mysterious name for the ghosts who haunted the ancient caves and crumbling cliff dwellings.

Through the years, the Anasazi have evolved. In the first half of the twentieth century, they were ancient, noble savages who eked out a hand-to-mouth living on the harsh, rainless plateaus of the arid Southwest. They were much like the Hopis and Zunis of the day—cultural relics of a bygone time, devoid of technical imagination and misguided in matters of religion. They could be pitied for having lived in that distant past and never knowing the Anglo cultural renaissance that would have put them in T-shirts and Chevrolets.

Then, as the twentieth century neared its end, the Ancient Ones evolved again. The Anasazi became hippies, like the new crop of professors who studied them. The former cliff dwellers were now perfect environmentalists who ran around blissfully naked and filled the canyons with beautiful music from their homemade flutes. Theirs was a non-materialistic culture of perfect peace and contentment. They lived in cliff-dwelling communes, grew organic food, and were surrounded by environmental harmony, universal brotherhood, and goodwill for all. They made beautiful pottery and wore sandals, beads, and flowers in their hair. They were the standard by which all people should live, a fine example of ancient peace, love, and enlightenment. The hippie park rangers at Mesa Verde told the tourists all about it.

And then archaeologists Christy Turner and Steven Le Blanc came along and blew the whole hippie-Anasazi connection out of the water. By studying ancient Indian bones, Turner was able to document brutality and cannibalism among the Anasazi. By studying ancient settlement patterns, Le Blanc was able to prove a multi-centuries pattern of strife and warfare across the whole of the American Southwest. It would seem that the Anasazi were not flower children after all. Bummer, dude.

And now, at the beginning of the twenty-first century, the Anasazi are evolving yet again. This time they are becoming activists. The Anasazi might be the key to winning court battles and land disputes between Native American tribes.

The primary focus so far has been an attempt to change the name of the tribe. By changing the term "Anasazi" to "Ancestral

Puebloans," activists seek to win a few court cases by swaying public perception and by making questionable cultural links to modern territories.

Some justify the proposed name change by alleging that the term "Anasazi"—which literally means "enemy ancestors," but has long been understood to mean "ancient people"—is demeaning to modern Pueblos. But the Pueblo objection might have more to do with the fact that the term is Navajo. The Navajos and Hopis have been locked in land disputes for many years. It is interesting to note that the Navajo National Historic Preservation Department (NNHPD) will reject any report sent to them for review if it uses the term "Ancestral Puebloan."

So the ancient Indians of the Moab area have had their name, culture, personality, worldview, politics, and tribal affiliation changed several times in the past 150 years, and they've been dead the whole time. We can only wonder who they might become in another forty years.

~ ~ ~

The Moki Scream

To those who have heard it, including the author of this book, the sound is unearthly. It starts as a low growl that quickly increases in pitch and volume until ending in a shriek. It's like no animal cry ever encountered and no bird call that has ever been heard. And the sound always seems to come from out of the dark.

Navajos have called it the Moki scream, and it will send cold fingers up your spine and frighten your breath away. You will wish you had a gun to defend yourself or a vehicle to escape in. Dogs will not challenge the sound, but will whimper, tuck their tails, and try to hide. Coyotes and crickets quit their nightly chorus and slink away, humbled and scared.

To the Navajo, a Moki is a dead person, one who haunts the cliff dwellings, canyons, and caves of the four-corners region. And when →

Ghost figures haunt the canyons of eastern Utah. Could they be the source of the Moki scream?

that shriek comes from out of a moonless night, it is easy to imagine a ghostly apparition with hollow eyes standing back in the junipers, challenging your very right to be there. Navajos avoid places like Indian ruins, where people have died and Mokis linger.

Some white men say the shriek is actually made by a mountain lion, a big cat out to find a mate and challenging others in his territory. But to someone hearing the sound in the middle of the night from a sleeping bag beneath a juniper tree, the fact that the scream might come from a lion is of small comfort. Cougars, ghosts, phantoms, spirits, warlocks, or witches—it's all the same when that Moki scream echoes through the canyons in the blackness of midnight. Pray that you never hear it.

~ ~ ~

The Earliest Artists of Moab

There is a distinct type of ancient rock art found only in eastern Utah. It is called Barrier Canyon Style, after the canyon where it was first scientifically studied. Barrier Canyon, also known as Horseshoe Canyon, is now a part of Canyonlands National Park. It is in the Robber's Roost, east of Highway U24 between the towns of Green River and Hanksville, a few miles west of Moab. The old cowboys called it Barrier Canyon because there was no good place it could be crossed on horseback.

The rock-art panels are quite rare. Only a few dozen are known to exist. The sites date back to the Archaic Culture, two thousand to eight thousand years ago.

The Archaic people were nomadic hunters and gatherers who lived in caves and rock shelters. They walked the canyons in a time before pottery, agriculture, and even the bow and arrow. They apparently made seasonal rounds of a large territory, where they harvested native plants and hunted with spears and atlatls (spear throwers).

Those nomads of the desert were masterful artists, too. Barrier Canyon rock art is generally more technically advanced, compositionally balanced, artistically mastered, and aesthetically powerful than anything that came after it. For that reason, it took a long time for some people to accept that Barrier Canyon Style is older than Fremont or Ute rock art traditions. But the evidence is irrefutable. At some sites, more recent Fremont Culture petroglyphs, dating from about AD 500 to 1300, are superimposed over the Barrier Canyon Style paintings.

Almost all examples of Barrier Canyon rock art are pictographs (painted panels) as opposed to petroglyphs (carved panels). And there are some distinct features that typify the style. The humanoid figures are often larger than life and are frequently referred to as "ghost

Two- to eight-thousand-year-old Barrier Canyon Style ghost figures near Thompson Springs (author photo)

figures." The figures usually have no arms or legs and appear to be spirits, ghosts, or gods—something beyond human. The figures often have huge, hollow eyes and a creepy appearance.

It has been suggested that the figures might represent ancient shamans who made transcendental journeys to the spirit world. There are often "spirit helpers," represented by small birds or animals that hover near the shoulders or face of the large, ghost-like images. The figures are usually dressed in long robes with intricate designs incised and painted to represent the fabric. Sometimes the paint has been scraped or rubbed into the sandstone with some type of tool, as if the artist was trying to work it deep into the porous rock, perhaps to make it last forever. The ghost figures are usually the central focus of the panels, but dogs, mountain sheep, and flowering plants are some-times depicted.

At the Horseshoe, or Barrier Canyon, site, "The Great Gallery" is quite possibly the single most impressive rock art site in the world. That's right—the world. The ghost figures are nine feet tall and painted in bright and varied colors with natural mineral pigments. "The Great Gallery" is accessible by a good but steep trail and a seven-mile round-trip hike.

Barrier Canyon panels are found over a wide area of eastern Utah, and Moab has a few. There is a good but faded panel at the mouth of Courthouse Wash, not far from Moab's river bridge, and a better site about forty miles north near the mouth of Sego Canyon, just a few miles above the town of Thompson Springs. A narrow but paved road goes right to the Sego Canyon site, and there are rest-room and picnic facilities there.

At the Sego Canyon site, a remarkable and powerful Barrier Canyon Style panel with several red ghost figures and dozens of other small elements graces an east-facing ledge. The ghost figures are not as large as at some other sites, but they are powerful just the same. To the south and just around the corner, high on the ledge, a row of faint Barrier Canyon figures is visible under Uintah-style Fremont figures that were superimposed later. The Fremont humanoids sport fancy necklaces and showy hairdos or headdresses. Just a little further to the west, in a shallow alcove, are some fine examples of Ute rock art, complete with horses. All three cultures are represented in one small area and accessible with a single stop and a very short hike.

Trailing Through Moab

The town of Moab sits firmly astride an ancient Indian trail. For countless years, Native Americans came to Moab to hunt, fish, trade, and cross the Colorado River. In the world of pre-history, the Colorado seems to have been a natural boundary between the Fremont Culture to the north and the Anasazi, or Ancestral Puebloans, to the south. In more recent times, the area was the home of Utes, Paiutes, and a few wandering Navajos.

No one remembers who the first Europeans were to see the Land of Moab, but Spaniards were in the area very early in the conquest of the Americas. Soldiers of the Coronado expedition discovered the Hopi towns in Arizona, the Grand Canyon, and the buffalo plains of Kansas as early as 1540. And for three hundred years thereafter, Spanish explorers made incursions into the four-corners area to explore and to trade with the natives. Most of those ventures were never recorded, but it is likely that some Spaniards were familiar with the Moab area by at least the mid-1600s.

The first recorded visit to Moab is that of Juan Rivera in 1765. Rivera was on an official reconnaissance and trading mission at the behest of the Spanish governor. He crossed the Colorado River near Moab to trade with Indians before returning to the Spanish settlements of New Mexico. Unfortunately, his account is only a brief outline of his adventures and few details are provided.

Spain controlled a vast territory in the New World, and her outposts were widely scattered. She had neither the population nor the means to adequately capitalize on the territory and resources she claimed. For centuries, most of the country remained free of Spanish settlements—a land of Indians, mystery, and legend. Many garden spots in the Southwest remained empty of European influence until after the Mexican War of 1848, when Americans poured in to fill the voids.

Spain also had colonies in California that were semi-isolated from the rest of the Spanish empire. California was a jewel in the Spanish crown, but she was hard to get to. Communication by sea was difficult in those early days before the Panama Canal. The Spaniards longed for an overland route from Mexico to California.

Early attempts to find such a route were foiled by the Grand Canyon. That great, impossibly deep gash in the earth's crust proved to be an impenetrable barrier. Exploring parties spent years trying to find a way through it or around it.

In July 1776, as the American colonies were declaring independence from England, Spanish priests Francisco Dominquez and Silvestre Velez de Escalante left Santa Fe, New Mexico, with eight other men to find a way around the Grand Canyon. Their destination was Monterey, California, and they kept a journal and made maps of their journey. The friars didn't visit the Land of Moab. They passed by a few miles to the east. But they gave us the first good account of what the country was like when it was wild and untamed. The journey of the padres was unsuccessful. After wandering in the wilderness for five months, they accepting defeat and returned to New Mexico. It would be left to others to open a road to California.

It is not known how it happened, but sometime between 1776 and 1830, a trail was blazed between Santa Fe and Los Angeles. It would become known in the annals of American history as the Old Spanish Trail. The route followed the ancient Indian trail through Moab and made use of the river crossing. Who made that first journey and the date it happened have been the subject of much

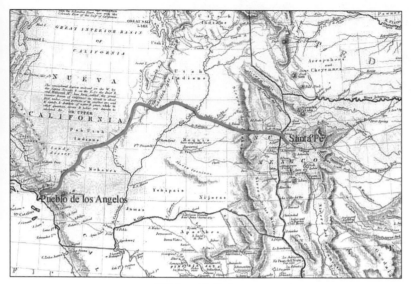

Old Spanish Trail map

speculation. There is an account of Spanish traders meeting Ute Indians in 1813 at a river crossing in Utah—at Moab or Green River)—"as was their custom," but there is no record that the trail to southern California was in operation at that date. Americans William Wolfskill and George Yount made the first recorded crossing of the entire Old Spanish Trail in 1830, but it is likely the Spaniards were using the trail long before that.

There is another account, though somewhat questionable, of a couple of "lost trappers," James Workman and Samuel Spencer, who journeyed down the Colorado River in 1810 and found a party of Spaniards camped near the river crossing at Moab. The Spaniards were on their way to California. If the story is true, Workman and Spencer were the first "Americans" to see the Land of Moab, and the Spanish Trail was open for business at least twenty years before Wolfskill and Yount made their journey.

In 1821 Mexico won her independence from Spain, and many of the Spanish restrictions on trade and travel among the natives were relaxed. By 1830 the Old Spanish Trail was a lively trade route, and the river crossing at Moab played a key role. Traders from New Mexico organized annual caravans. Dozens of merchants packed woolen goods on mules for the twelve-hundred-mile journey to southern California. The entire road was a pack trail and not suited for wagons or carts. In California the merchants traded serapes and blankets for horses and mules that were then herded back over the trail to New Mexico. It was a lucrative trading venture that benefited both the California settlements and the New Mexicans.

But there was a dark side to the caravan trade, too—a stain on the history of the Old Spanish Trail.

Trading Gone Wrong

The Ute Indians, being great entrepreneurs in those early days, were quick to take advantage of the trading opportunities. They traded peltries to the Spanish merchants and soon discovered that the traders were eager to buy slaves. The institution of slavery was well established in the new world at that time, prospering in Mexico as well as the American colonies. Both the Spanish, and later the Mexicans, bought young women and children from the Utes and resold the captives in the settlements at both ends of the trail.

The Utes had horses and guns and were more powerful than their Paiute cousins, who lived an ancient, hunting-and-gathering way of life. The Utes began to raid the hapless Paiutes, hunting them down like rabbits, stealing women and children to sell to the traders. Some caravan merchants, too, joined in the hunt for Paiutes as they passed through the territory. The slave trade flourished in southern Utah for at least twenty years, and might have lasted for more than fifty years—no one knows for sure. The Paiute culture of southern Utah and Nevada was decimated. Many Paiutes not captured and sold into slavery starved to death while hiding from Utes and slave traders far from the fertile valleys and marshes that sustained their way of life.

At the end of the Mexican War in 1848, Americans closed the Old Spanish Trail to Mexican traders, but parts of it were still heavily used by Americans. Some parts became modern highways. Highway 191 follows the old slave trail from a point near Interstate 70, south through Moab to Monticello, and then highway 666 continues the route into southern Colorado.

the slave trade officially ended with the closing of the Old Spanish Trail, but there is evidence that it continued for a few more years. There is a famous story in Utah of a powerful Ute chieftain named Arapeen who brought a few Paiute children to the town of Provo as late as 1853 and tried to sell them to the Mormons. When the townspeople refused to buy the children, Arapeen grabbed one child by the feet and dashed its head against the ground, killing the little one. He then told the Mormons they were heartless for not buying the child and saving its life.

No caravans of slave traders have crossed the Utah desert since 1848, but there are said to be ghosts who still walk the Old Spanish Trail. Find a quiet place in the canyons near Moab, listen carefully, and you might hear an old Paiute crying for her children.

Called to the Land

T he first Europeans to settle the great state of Utah came west with Brigham Young in 1847. From the American perspective of that time, the West was open and empty. Native Americans didn't count. The land was free for the taking.

The Mormon migration to Utah is one of the great epics of the American West. Tens of thousands of faithful members of the Church of Jesus Christ of Latter-day Saints sold everything in Europe and the eastern United States to cross the American plains to settle the great interior basin beyond the Rocky Mountains. They came in covered

t he Mormons called it the Territory of Deseret and hoped to make it the State of Deseret after the United States claimed the region following the Mexican War of 1848. The word "deseret" is a word from the *Book of Mormon* that is said to mean "honeybee." The honeybee is still Utah's official state insect and the beehive an official state emblem. Utah Highway Patrol troopers have beehives on their uniforms and the doors of their patrol cars.

wagons and on foot pulling handcarts. And once the church was firmly rooted in the valley of the Great Salt Lake, Brigham Young envisioned a great earthly "Kingdom of God" that would encompass the whole of the Great Basin and parts of the Colorado Plateau. The proposed kingdom would cover a vast area that included all of present Utah and Nevada, with parts of Idaho, Wyoming, Colorado, New Mexico, Arizona, and California included.

In the beginning, the Territory of Deseret was an ambitious undertaking, even for the ever-optimistic Brigham Young. Originally he had only a few thousand followers to protect his borders and legitimize his claim to the land. But in spite of scant numbers, he immediately set out on a mission to occupy the best land available to strengthen his hold and to discourage non-Mormon settlers.

From 1847 onward, an ever-expanding number of Mormon settlements spread out through the valleys and desert glens of the Great Basin as Mormon converts migrated to Utah and were immediately put to work building the kingdom. Eventually, from the home base at Salt Lake City, Mormon colonists would claim places as far removed as southeast Idaho, northern Arizona, Las Vegas, and San Bernardino, California.

Brigham Young's practice of sending colonists to claim the more fertile parts of the wilderness became a religious obligation to his followers. Church members were "called" and "set apart" by religious ordination as colonizing missionaries. Their mission was to claim the land in an area specifically assigned to them, and there build prosperous farms, ranches, and communities. A secondary, but important, part of the "calling" was to befriend the native peoples and convert them to Christian Mormonism.

The Elk Mountain Mission of 1855 was Brigham Young's first attempt at colonizing the red rock county of southeastern Utah, and the present site of Moab was the place selected for the first settlement. Some historians have said that one purpose of the mission might have been to establish a Mormon presence along the Old Spanish Trail. The trail was a back door to the Territory of Deseret, and there were no settlements to guard the door and keep track of who was passing through—and he who controlled the Old Spanish Trail controlled commerce over a vast area of the American Southwest.

As was the Mormon custom, Brigham Young sent a scouting party to ascertain the lay of the land and select a site for the settlement. In 1854 twelve men—eleven Mormon Elders and an Indian guide—were sent from settlements in central Utah to explore the area near the Elk Mountains where the Old Spanish Trail crossed the Colorado River.

The exploring party took the first wagons to the area. Part of their mission was to open a wagon road that could be used by colonizers who would follow sometime later. The explorers followed the Old Spanish Trail through eastern Utah to the Colorado River. At the bottom of Moab Canyon, near the present entrance to Arches National Park, the party had to dismantle their wagons and lower them with ropes down a twenty-five-foot "jumping-off place" on the sandstone rim. The jumping-off place could be seen for many years, but has since been blasted away to make room for widening the highway.

After crossing the river at the Old Spanish Crossing, the explorers were favorably impressed with the location and fertile soil of the future site of Moab. In their report back to Brigham Young, they recommended the

Iater, the name Elk Mountains, which originated with the Native Americans, would be changed to La Sal Mountains, a name used by early Spaniards. It is said that Spanish explorers could not believe that the white caps on the mountains could be snow. In such a hot country, it surely had to be salt. And as if to confirm the supposition, the Indians showed them salt deposits at the base of the mountains. Hence the name was recorded on Spanish maps as Sierra de La Sal—the Mountains of Salt.

valley as a place for settlement. It was a great location. The valley had clean, flowing water, rich soil, timber in the nearby mountains, and much sage and pinion for firewood and fences. The site was also smack dab in the center of the Old Spanish Trail and right at the river crossing. It was everything Brigham Young had hoped for.

A colonizing party of forty-one men was "called" and "set apart" by church leaders the following spring. The venture was named the Elk Mountain Mission. In May 1855, the men left the Mormon settlements with fifteen wagons, sixty-five oxen, thirteen horses, sixteen cows, two bulls, one calf, two pigs, four dogs, and twelve chickens. They set out for Little Grand Valley (Spanish Valley) on the Old Spanish Trail. Their purpose was to pioneer a settlement and then return to collect their families after some of the heavy work had been completed. It was thought that women and children might be an impediment in the early months of clearing fields, digging irrigation ditches, and building a fort for protection. Leaving the women behind, as the church leaders counseled, proved to be a wise decision. The colonists made a wagon road around the "jumping-off" place near the bottom of Moab Canyon, crossed the river, and reached their destination on June 15, 1855.

Building on Shaky Ground

T he colonists immediately set to work preparing the ground for crops and building a fort. The fort was a stone enclosure sixty-four feet square with walls twelve feet high. Small cabins within the walls sheltered the men from the elements and—hopefully—from the slings and arrows of cruel misfortune. The settlers would need their fort in the weeks to come.

The site of the old Mormon fort was very near where Moab's Motel 6 is located today. The old fort was west of Highway 191 at about 900 North. Sadly, nothing remains of the Mormon fort, and there is nothing to see at the site. A monument was erected near the location some years ago, but was removed recently to make way for widening of the highway. The monument can now be seen in front of the Daughters of the Utah Pioneers building at 200 East and about 50 North, just behind the old pioneer Star Theatre.

At first things progressed well for the Elk Mountain Mission. The colonists dug ditches, cleared land, and planted crops. Work on the fort progressed nicely. Surprisingly, there was a noticeable lack of Indians in the area. The valley was known to be a trading ground and a meeting place for Utes and Paiutes who lived in the neighborhood, but no tribe claimed exclusive rights to the area.

But slowly the Indians began to appear. They came in small groups at first and then became a flood of curious onlookers eager to see the pale newcomers. All of them wanted to trade. The Mormons did a brisk business in the Indian trade. They got rich in horses while foolishly trading guns, powder, and lead to the unpredictable "wild men of the desert." The settlers had brought with them ninety-nine pounds of gun powder, two hundred pounds of lead, and more than thirty-seven thousand percussion caps for the black powder firearms of the day. The natives were delighted to have a ready source of the white man's goods at their disposal, but they could have done without the white men.

A forewarning of the Indian sentiment became apparent when a regional Ute chieftain visited the missionaries. His name was Quit-sub-soc-its, which the Mormons quickly shortened to St. John. The newly renamed Chief St. John demanded "great" presents from the settlers for being presumptuous enough to have claimed the land as their own. The emissaries of Brigham Young mollified the chief by giving him a blanket, two shirts, a hearty meal, some tobacco, and kind words around the campfire.

Two weeks later, Chief St. John spoke at a "public meeting." He told the missionaries that he had told his people to treat the Mormons well, but he put the settlers on notice that there were plenty of white men in the valley already. He didn't want them to bring any more. The Utes had already been chased out of their fertile, ancestral valleys to the west by encroaching white settlements, and they were beginning to see the writing on the wall.

The Elk Mountain Missionaries were conscientious in their efforts to make friends with the natives, and only a month after their arrival, they baptized fifteen Indians and ordained four of them as Mormon Elders. It is doubtful that the natives understood the full meaning of the ceremonies, having been taught the gospel through hand signals and interpreters, but the Indians understood that the action made them friends and "brothers" of the missionaries. In a world of constantly warring tribes, slave traders, white encroachment, and ever-looming starvation, powerful friends were a good thing.

But relations with the natives began to deteriorate as the settlers' crops began to ripen. The Indians just couldn't deny themselves a ripe melon, a fine squash, or a tender ear of ripening corn. They helped themselves to the Mormon gardens, much to the consternation of the settlers. When rebuked for their thievery, the natives became angry and sullen.

And then, in a move they would soon regret, the leaders of the settlement allowed twenty-one of the forty-one missionaries to return to the Mormon settlements to visit their families before the onset of winter. The Indians saw advantage in the reduced number of whites and they became very "saucy and impudent," according to one colonist's journal. To make matters even worse, the Mormons had made a killing in the horse-trading business that summer and were low on trade goods by then. And as winter approached and their gardens were being constantly raided, they were less inclined to share food. The charm of the newcomers was beginning to wear thin for the natives.

The Decline and Fall
of the Elk Mountain Mission

I n late September, a Ute named "Charles," a son of Chief St.
John, shot and killed one of the Mormons when the man was
away from the fort attempting to catch a horse. Once that
deed was done, the natives figured they were in big trouble with the
settlers and had nothing to loose by attacking the fort. They came
with a vengeance. The guns, powder, and lead the missionaries had
traded for horses came back to haunt them.

Two of the Mormons had been out hunting on Elk Mountain, and
they were ambushed and gunned down as they returned to the fort
later that same day. The Indians made off with their guns and horses.
With three men killed and another wounded, the Mormons were in a
tight situation within the walls of their fort. The Indians burned
haystacks and set fire to outbuildings. But the whites were not slack-
ers when it came to shooting. They got a few of the Indians in that
first encounter.

Through the late afternoon and evening, the missionaries and the
Indians yelled back and forth as they shot at each other. The
Mormons offered peace, but the natives demanded revenge for their
dead and wounded. Finally, it was agreed that the natives would go
home for the night and leave the Mormons alone if the whites would

toss all of their bread out of the fort to the Indians. The deed was done. For a few loaves of bread, the missionaries bought a few hours respite from the fighting. But the natives promised to return in the morning and continue where they had left off. To the colonists' practical and properly programmed Anglo-Saxon minds, the Native American mindset and rules of war must have been true enigmas.

The next morning, shooting and negotiations began again. Incredibly, the Mormons were able to buy safe passage across the river by giving the natives six cows. Unfortunate for them, they also had to abandon five horses and twenty-five other cattle that they were unable to round up.

The missionaries left their fort, most of their belongings, and the bodies of their three friends to the mercy of the Indians. It is said that a friendly Indian, probably one of the aboriginal Mormon Elders, helped the missionaries get away. The "good Indian" also promised to return to the battle site and bury the three slain Mormons. Folklore has it that the bodies were buried within the walls of the old fort.

The missionaries beat a hasty retreat back to the safety of northern Utah and never went back to reclaim the land of their sacred church calling. The Elk Mountain Mission was one of only a few failures in the colonizing efforts of Brigham Young. To the Mormons, the Land of Moab was a wild place beyond taming. It would be left to other men, less pious and tougher, to bring the natives and the land to heel.

By running off the Mormons, the Indians bought themselves another generation—22 years—of freedom and undisputed ownership of the Moab area. It would be 1877 before another white man would live in the old Mormon fort. And then, that white man would be a black man.

"Negro Bill" and Frenchie

After the retreat of the Elk Mountain Missionaries in the fall of 1855, there is scant evidence of white men being in the Moab area for several years. It is known that trappers and prospectors, outlaws and Indians, moved through the area along the Old Spanish Trail, but there are few records.

A man named Crispen Taylor was one of the first white men to make an attempt at cattle ranching in the Moab area. Taylor scouted the area in 1874 and took a herd of cows there in 1875. But he was quickly chased out by Indians. The country must have impressed him, for he returned six years later and stayed.

Two other cowboys—the Green brothers, Silas and George—also took cows into the Moab area in 1875. The Green brothers stayed in spite of the Indians, and both died—or were killed—during the winter of 1876–77. In the spring of 1877, a search party found the body of Silas in the upper Spanish Valley. He had been dead for some time. Members of the search party said it looked as if he had been dragged by his feet, because his shirt was up around his head. His brother was never found.

It was never proven that Indians killed either of the Green brothers, but Indians have always shouldered the blame. There was a rumor that George might have drowned in the river, and it's possible that Silas was dragged to death in an accident with his horse. The truth is still a mystery, but murder by wild Indians has made the Green brothers' disappearance a great campfire story for more than one hundred years.

Actually, as cowboys and adventurous new settlers sneaked back into the Moab area after twenty years of avoiding the place, there is little mention of Indians—at least not in the way they were talked about in the 1850s. Indian numbers seem to have dropped significantly between 1855 and 1877.

There could be several reasons for the lower numbers of Indians. In the 1860s, reservations were established in Colorado and Arizona for the Utes and the Navajos. And while several small bands of Utes and Paiutes remained wild and free in the Moab area, most of the natives had gone to the agencies, where they could receive free food and clothing. It is also probable that inter-tribal warfare and white-man diseases reduced the numbers even more. As new settlers began to arrive, they did find some Indians in their various tribes and linguistic divisions, but the natives didn't have the numbers to be a threat like they had been some twenty years earlier. The days of free-ranging, wild Indians were almost over in the American West.

In early 1877, about the same time cowboy search parties were out looking for the bodies of the Green brothers, two prospectors wandered into the Land of Moab and took up residency in the Old Mormon Fort. One was a mysterious Frenchman who kept his name as well hidden as his past. The other was William Granstaff, a black man who became famous in eastern Utah as "Negro Bill." Actually, a much rougher term than "Negro" was used to describe the man until the civil-rights era of the 1960s.

The two men came to the area together, sharing a single burro to pack their camp equipment. They were friends, but not good friends, and they didn't live together. They divided the fort and Spanish Valley into two equal parts. It is said they might have starved to death that first winter had it not been for a few of the Green brothers' cows they found wandering about the valley. The fact that unclaimed domestic cattle were roaming the valley without being appropriated by Indians tells a lot about the status of the Indians at the time.

Recognizing an opportunity, Bill went into the cow business. A few years later, as new settlers came to the valley, Bill told them he owned about 40 head of "horned stock." He kept his cows in a canyon east of Moab that is marked on maps today as "Negro Bill Canyon."

Bill and Frenchie, as the Frenchman was known, planted a big garden and eked out a primitive existence at the old fort for a time. One story has them trading garden vegetables for flour and other staples from new settlers and passersby. They tended a few cows, caught a few fish, and hunted and trapped in the mountains like the Indians. But as new pioneers arrived, the place got too crowded for Frenchie.

In 1878 the Frenchman sold his half of Spanish Valley to A.G. Wilson, a potential farmer and homesteader. But when Wilson returned that fall with his family and homesteading tools, he found that Frenchie had also sold the land to Walter Moore, another homesteader. Fortunately, the two men decided there was land enough for both of them, and they divided the property equitably. Frenchie had, in the meantime, escaped "down the river to trap." With that, the mysterious Frenchman disappears from the annals of the Land of Moab. He was never seen or heard from again. Who he was, where he came from, and where he went with the homesteaders' money is one of those quaint mysteries of the canyon country.

"Negro Bill" Granstaff minded his own business, tended his cows, and stayed at his ranch and small cabin in the canyon until after an Indian uprising known in the literature as the Pinhook Massacre of 1881 (more on that to come). Indians killed more than a dozen settlers at the time, and white sentiment toward the natives was murderous. Being a member of a despised minority himself, Bill saw the ugly mood, recognized the potential for senseless violence, and decided it was time to hit the trail. It is also said that some had accused him of selling whiskey to the natives and "stirring up the troubles."

Before he left, Bill told a friend, "The men are gathering guns to go on the mountain to hunt Indians, but I think I'm the Indian they are after." With that, he saddled his horse and left the area forever. Others would soon take possession of his cabin and the quiet canyon that still bears his name. A man named Art Taylor reported seeing old "Negro Bill" Granstaff three years later in Salida, Colorado. The former Utah pioneer, rancher, and big-time landowner was shining shoes for a living.

Modern Moab Takes Shape

Eighteen seventy-eight was the year the floodgates of white settlement were opened to the area around Moab. Free land for homesteading was becoming scarce in the more settled regions, and the frontier was expanding. People were turning to more marginal and harder-to-conquer lands, places that had been bypassed or overlooked when better land was available. Moab was such a place, and several homesteaders came to the area in 1878 hoping to put down roots in the red desert soil.

By 1878, Negro Bill and Frenchie had been living at the Old Mormon Fort for a year, and they served as a welcoming committee. Most of the newcomers stopped at their place for a day—or a month or two—and ate squash and corn from the black man's garden while exploring the area for good sites to homestead. At least a half dozen pioneer families came that year. Some settled in Spanish Valley, but others pushed on to greener pastures near the future town of La Sal.

Some of the earliest pioneers settled in upper Spanish Valley at a place they named Plainfield. Plainfield had the promise and potential to be the dominant settlement in the area, and it was granted a post office in late 1879, a few months before Moab had a post office. A few years later, the name was changed to Bueno (Spanish for "good"), but the hopeful name couldn't change the fate or the fortunes of the community. The farms and fields slowly dried up and blew away. By the early years of the twentieth century, the locals were calling the place Poverty Flats, a name that still endures. Eventually, Poverty Flats was abandoned, and the farmers moved lower into the valley near Moab.

Eighteen seventy-nine brought another migration of at least six more families who settled in the area. By 1880 there were enough people living in the lower valley to warrant a post office, and the Land of Moab was officially christened with a name. That same year, Moab became a part of newly created Emery County, Utah.

Eighteen eighty-one was another big year for immigration, with the extended Taylor families—eleven adults and twenty children—and others arriving to stake claims in the lower valley. By the winter of 1881–82, the citizens of Moab pooled their labor and resources to construct a log building to serve as a school and a meetinghouse. A town was beginning to take shape.

Most of the early settlers camped in tents or wagon boxes while preparing the land for a homestead. It was more important to dig ditches, make corrals and fences, and plow fields than to build a house. The settlers were a long way from any store or source of supplies, and the success of the venture depended on the crop in the ground and the well-being of the livestock. People came second, and that was never more evident than in the makeup of the family dwellings.

Home, Sweet (?) Home

A settler's first home in the wilderness was usually a crude, temporary cabin built to provide shelter and not comfort. A year or two later, after the farm or ranch was beginning to prosper, the family would turn its efforts to making a more substantial log, rock, or mud-brick home.

Often, the first temporary house was a dugout—a cabin built into a bank of dirt or a hillside. A dugout was a cheap and easy way to build a cabin, especially in the western states, where logs were scarce and it didn't rain often. By digging into a hill with a pick and shovel, a pioneer could use three sides of the excavation for the walls of the structure. This cut down on lumber as well as labor. Only the front of the structure had to be "built up" using logs or rocks. The cabin was then roofed over with logs, willows, cedar bark, grass, dirt, and sometimes even flat rocks. A fireplace was built somewhere in the structure if the family was too poor to own an iron stove.

One advantage of a dugout was that it had natural air-conditioning and insulation. A dugout was usually warmer in winter and cooler in summer than a regular log cabin. True, a prolonged rain might weaken the structure or bury it with mud washing down from the hill above, but such were the hazards of life in the wilderness. Dugouts were primitive survival shelters and not real houses.

A pioneer dugout cabin in eastern Utah
(author photo)

Furniture was scant in the first wave of settlement to a new area. Wagon boxes were small and space was needed for tools, bedding, foodstuffs, seeds, and survival equipment. There was no room for kitchen tables, china closets, or pianos. Those items would be shipped in later when the roads had been improved and a better house built. In the early years of tents and dugouts, the furniture was rough, homemade, and field expedient. Rough-cut boards were nailed or tied together to make tables and benches. Beds were made by lapping a rope back and forth around horizontal poles and covering the lashing with a featherbed or a sack stuffed with straw.

Water was usually obtained by dipping a bucket into a nearby river, stream, or irrigation ditch. In many places in eastern Utah, wells are not practical because of the nature of the soil and the brackishness of sub-surface water. Most pioneers in Utah used surface water of some kind. And in an age when people knew little about microbes and parasites, it is not surprising that hundreds of early pioneers died from water-borne diseases. Cholera and dysentery were common on the frontier.

Sanitation was always a problem in most early homesteads. With frequently substandard water, homemade soap, clothing that was not often laundered, and poor facilities for bathing and personal hygiene, most pioneers smelled pretty ripe. A simple wash pan and a rag were often the best a pioneer woman could offer.

Latrines were crude outhouses, a simple hole in the ground, or a special place in the bushes near the cabin. Chamber pots were used at night when a trip to the outhouse might be interrupted by snakes, bugs, critters with teeth and claws, or wild Indians. In the days before Sears catalogs, toilet paper might be cornhusks, finely shredded cedar bark, or even cottonwood leaves.

The early homesteaders often looked down on the Indians as being dirty, but in reality, the natives, who wore few items of clothing and moved their camps every few days or weeks, were probably, as a group, much cleaner and healthier than most of the early white settlers. Even the cowboys, often dressed like the dandies of the West in books and movies, wore their clothing and carried the tools of their trade for utility, not looks. The glamorous West was anything but.

The Marlboro Men of Moab

anching was also big business in the early years of Moab. Most homesteaders kept a few cows for milk, meat, and trading material, and there were several big cattle ranches in the area. One of the bigger spreads was the Carlisle Cattle Company, an outfit that ran thousands of cattle on the Blue Mountains south of Moab in the 1880s. It was the Carlisle Ranch that hired many of the Texas cowboys who played a prominent role in the history of Grand and San Juan counties. The infamous Tom Roach and good guy "Latigo" Gordon were two of the best-known Carlisle employees.

Al Scorup and his Scorup-Somerville Cattle Company was another large ranching operation that ranged cattle over a

Latigo Gordon is thought to have been the model for Zane Grey's "Lassiter" in the cowboy classic *Riders of the Purple Sage*, first published in 1912. The Moab landscape and Moab cowboys provided much inspiration for Zane Grey's popular western novels in the early part of the twentieth century.

Patterson cabin in Lisbon Valley with cowgirl and cowboys, 1915
(Museum of Moab photo PR-1)

large area that included much of what would become Canyonlands National Park.

Cowboying on the desert has always been a tough business. In the 1800s, there were few roads, and everything was done on horseback. Pack trains carried supplies to distant cowboy line camps and then took sick, injured, and lonesome cowboys back out to civilization. Cowboys were often isolated for months at a time, sometimes sleeping in caves or Indian ruins as they followed the cows to water and grass.

Everyone carried a gun in the early days. It was a tool for protection from Indians, outlaws, wild animals, or even a wild-eyed old cow. It was also a signaling device in those days before cell phones and walkie-talkies. Guns make a loud noise in the canyons, and a lonesome cowboy might use one to signal a partner as to his whereabouts.

For many years, a universal signal of distress was three quick shots, a pause, and then three quick shots again.

Like Arabs of the Middle East, the cowboys of eastern Utah wore a lot of clothing in the hot climate. In the 1800s, long-john cotton underwear was considered to be a necessity. Anything less was barbaric and uncivilized. The cowboys also wore long-sleeved shirts, heavy denim pants, wide felt hats, and often a vest, chaps, and a bandanna around the neck. The heavy clothing provided protection from bugs, dust, and thorn bushes, as well as the sun.

a cowboy's diet was often limited to items that wouldn't spoil and that could be packed around for weeks in a saddlebag—sourdough biscuits, salt pork, beans, cornmeal, cheese, coffee, and 30-30 bullets. They didn't eat the bullets. Cowboys hunted as they tended the cows, often shooting deer, elk, or antelope for food.

david Lavender, in his wonderful book *One Man's West*, tells of seeing a group of Al Scorup's cowboys skinny-dipping in a stock pond at the Dugout Ranch near Moab. He says the contrast of skin tones was shocking. The cowboys all had very dark, suntanned faces, necks, and hands, but the rest of their bodies were stark white from never being exposed to the sun.

Even a cowboy's face was two-toned. From the eyebrows down, the face was a weather-beaten reddish-brown, but the forehead was fish-belly white from always being covered by a hat. Sometimes the line separating the two colors of the face was as pronounced as if it had been drawn with a pencil.

Pioneer women, too, wore a lot of clothing for living on the desert. Bloomers, petticoats, long skirts that touched the ground, and aprons were the fashion of the day. Dresses and blouses all had long sleeves, and every woman wore a sunbonnet with a wrap-around face shade. It was unbecoming for a woman to have suntanned skin.

And most women of the day wouldn't be caught dead wearing men's clothing. Those foxy frontier babes who wear Gucci jeans in the modern cowboy movies are only figments of some screen-writer's imagination. Proper ladies

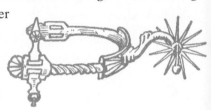

rode a horse sidesaddle in skirts. Indian women and cowgirls were considered heathens for straddling a horse. Cultured and refined white women of the Victorian age rode in horse-drawn carriages with their knees properly together and their skirts tucked modestly around their legs.

Spurs and leather cuffs around the wrists were tools of the cowboy trade. Spurs made a horse pay attention and step lively, and leather cuffs protected a cow-boy's wrists from rope burns. Ropes were haz-ards as well as useful

high-heeled boots were a safety feature that helped to keep a cowboy's feet from becoming entangled in the stirrup of his saddle. And some old cow-boys couldn't walk barefooted after wearing nothing but high-heeled boots all of their lives. The high heels would shrink the Achilles tendon, and it was painful—or even impossible—for the old boys to get by in slippers or low-heeled shoes. More than one old cowboy went to the Old Folks Home still wearing his high-heeled work boots. He couldn't walk any other way.

tools, and most cowboys who had been in the business for a few years were missing fingers or thumbs. One of the most common of cowboy accidents was to wrap a finger against the saddle horn when roping cows. The horn on a stock saddle is used to secure the rope when dragging cows and calves around, and with a thousand-pound horse on one end of the rope and a nine-hundred-pound steer on the other end, a finger caught by the rope against a saddle horn was quickly amputated. An old cowboy who had been in the business for twenty or thirty years usually couldn't count to eight using the fingers and thumbs of both hands. The famous Latigo Gordon was missing all four fingers on one hand.

A River Runs Past It

In 1776 the river that runs past Moab was drawn on Father Escalante's map and labeled the Rio De Los Zaguaganas (River of the Zaguaganas tribe). The name referred to a group of Indians the padres found living along the riverbank in what would one day be Colorado. Escalante named a few rivers for Indian tribes during his travels. The San Juan River he called the Rio De Nabajoo in honor of the tribe that calls Monument Valley home today.

Father Escalante's name for Moab's river did not endure for long. In the early days of American westward expansion, it became known as the Grand River (or Rio Grande in Spanish). The Grand began in the mountains of central Colorado, flowed down through eastern Utah, and joined the Green River south of Moab to form the mighty Colorado.

But in the early years of the twentieth century, the State of Colorado claimed the Grand River as her own. The Colorado congressional delegation petitioned Congress to change the name of the Grand River to the Colorado River, and in July 1921, the deed was done. The Grand became the upper reaches of the Colorado. The only vestiges of the original name remain with Grand Junction, Colorado, where the Grand and Gunnison Rivers joined, and Grand County,

Route of the Dominguez-Escalante Expedition

Utah, where Moab is the county seat.

For many years, Moab was the only good place to cross the river between Mack, Colorado, and Cass Hite's Dandy Crossing, about 150 miles downstream. The river crossing made Moab a destination. Early cowboy and Indian trails bottlenecked at Moab's riverbanks.

In the early days, crossing the river was an adventure. There was no bridge or ferryboat—and in fact, there was seldom any type of boat to use at all. People got wet crossing the river, and most crossed au naturel. Wet clothing and boots full of water could get a person killed if he had to swim.

Indians took to the water astride cottonwood logs or made crude boats of willows and hide. Trappers used rafts lashed together with

Pioneers had a difficult time getting their livestock across the river, too. One story tells of crossing the Green River when the cows refused to swim across. When the dim-bulbed bovines were forced into the water with horses and whips, they simply swam in circles, following each other. Finally the men had to pull several across the river by tying them to a boat and dragging them through the water while the other cows played "follow the leader" and paddled along behind.

ropes or rawhide. Cowboys hit the water still in the saddle, trusting a good horse to carry them across. Pioneers floated wagons across with logs tied to the sides like primitive outriggers. Livestock swam, animals and people drowned, and pioneer women swooned at the very thought of a big river crossing. Death by drowning was one of the primary hazards of touring the Land of Moab in those early days.

For a few weeks each season the river was low, and fording the channel could be accomplished with relative ease and safety. At other times the water ran high, and the need to cross was measured carefully against the odds. Sometimes the risk was just too great. People often camped by the river for days or weeks waiting for lower water that would give them a better chance to survive the crossing. Many people drowned anyway, and the literature is full of stories of trappers, settlers, and early explorers losing all of their worldly goods to the river.

A Ferry Good Idea

hen Norman Taylor and his family first arrived at Moab in October 1881, they saw the bodies of two men who had drowned while attempting to cross the river just the day before. That tragedy might have prompted Taylor to build Moab's first ferryboat. Taylor was a practical man, too. He saw a good business opportunity in helping weary travelers brave the horrors of the river.

The first ferryboat was a twenty-eight-foot, oar-powered craft that was best suited for carrying people and light cargo. Wagons had to be dismantled and ferried across in pieces. Livestock was still required to swim, but for the first time ever, pioneer women were able to cross the river without getting their long skirts and ringlets wet.

Later, in about 1884, a more seaworthy, sixty-foot ferryboat was built that could be pulled across the river by means of cables and ropes. Then whole wagons and teams could be ferried in relative comfort over the dark and rolling waves. The ferry existed with modifications and mishaps for many years. Taylor eventually leased the ferry to other operators, and finally it was purchased by Grand County and operated as a public-owned conveyance.

Moab's spirit of entrepreneurship and willingness to make a buck from the traveling public developed early at that watery gate to the

Ferryboat at Moab, 1900–1910. This is one of the few photos of Henry Grimm (third from the right in long coat), famed Moab blacksmith. The pasture across the road from Henry's shop was known as Monkey Wrench Pasture because Henry had a violent temper and was always throwing his tools out the door, some of which landed in this pasture, located just south of the junction of Mill Creek Drive and 4th East. (Museum of Moab photo 17-23)

community. Faun McConkie Tanner, in her history of Moab, *The Far Country*, tells of old timers who remembered a sign hanging on the old ferryboat. It is alleged to have said: "We accommodate to accumulate. In God we trust—all others spot cash." In fact, when the county took control of the ferry in 1897, they lowered the fare from $2.50 to 50 cents per wagon.

In January 1911, state money was appropriated to build a bridge over the river at Moab. The 620-foot, triple-span, single-lane steel structure was completed in 1912 at a cost of $43,000. A dollar bought a lot of bridge in 1912.

On April 8, 1912, Grand County hosted a celebration honoring the opening of the bridge. It is said that thirteen hundred people attended the festivities, a large chunk of the populations of Grand and San Juan counties at the time. There was food and drink, speeches, politicking, and congratulations all around. And then many of the old-timers promenaded across the new bridge to give a figurative finger to the cold, dark water that had vexed them for so long. Moab finally had a proper gateway.

The first bridge served faithfully until the 1950s, when the narrow, single-lane structure proved to be inadequate for ever-increasing traffic and the heavy trucks of the mining industry. In 1955 a new two-lane bridge was constructed and still serves the community today. The foundations of the northern approach to the old bridge can still be seen about two hundred yards upstream from the current bridge. And in times of low water, remnants of the old bridge pilings can be seen in mid-channel.

With the opening of the bridge in 1912, Moab entered the modern world. It is interesting to note that many historians count 1912 as the year the American frontier officially came to a close. With a new river bridge, Moab and the rest of eastern Utah began a new era.

It would be wrong to call it a portent of things to come, but a Grand County newspaper story

from today's perspective, it is hard to understand the full significance of having a bridge across the river. At the time of its completion, the Moab Bridge was the only bridge over the Colorado River between Grand Junction, Colorado, and Needles, California. The bridge transformed all of southeastern Utah. Initially, electricity and telephones didn't have a bigger impact on the community.

The first river bridge at Moab, completed in 1912 and used until 1955
(Museum of Moab photo 34-13)

of 1912 began with the headline, "Bridge is Perpect." Surely a young typesetter had a tough time living down that misspelling, but "Perpect" pretty well summed things up for the whole community. Things have never been perfect in Moab. The town has always had to struggle.

The Pinhook "Massacre"

By the time the first settlers were making cabins and digging irrigation ditches in the Moab area in the late 1870s, most of the Indians still in the area were considered to be "renegades" by the whites. Reservations had been established for both Utes and Navajos in the 1860s, and renegades were holdouts who refused to leave the land of their ancestors. The natives had occupied the land since the beginning of time, and they saw no reason to eat salt pork and crackers on a reservation while deer and antelope still played in eastern Utah.

The renegade bands were often a mixed bunch, consisting of Utes, Paiutes, and Navajos. When facing a common enemy, ancient tribal rivalries were sometimes put aside in the interests of survival. Small bands of outlaw Indians frequented the less-settled parts of the land, hiding in the shadows while practicing the "old ways" for another year or another season.

The whites seem to have had some small measure of tolerance for the renegades as long as competition for land, water, game, and grass did not become too stiff. For a few years, into the late 1870s, the Indians and early homesteaders kept a troubled peace. The non-reservation Indians still traded with the whites, and most were not bashful about showing up at a settler's cabin to ask for food or small presents of tobacco and cloth as small token payments for the land the cabin was sitting on. Most ranchers and homesteaders complied with the requests to avoid conflict.

But the settlers were never tolerant when hungry natives killed a cow to replace the deer and elk that had once been plentiful. The Indians had a tough time understanding the white man's concept of privately owned land and privately owned free-ranging cows. Conflicts were inevitable between the two cultures.

Serious Indian troubles began in September 1879 when Utes on the White River Indian Agency, a reservation in Colorado, revolted. Indian agent Nathan Meeker had decided to make farmers out of people who knew only hunting and gathering as a way of life, and he became a little too forceful with his demands. His agricultural students rebelled, killing him and seven of his agency workers. They also killed a few soldiers sent to restore order. Under threat of hanging or severe sanctions, many of the Utes did the prudent thing and headed for the hills. They fled the reservation, hooking up with various small bands of renegades already out in the wilds.

Unfortunately, things had changed on the old Ute stomping grounds. In the few years the Indians had been away, white men had claimed most of the good spots, and most of the wild game was gone. Gold had been discovered in southern Colorado, and swarms of prospectors were out and about. It was a tough situation for people accustomed to living off the land.

Hunger, fear of reprisals if they went back to the agency, and frustration at finding every hidden valley stocked with white man's cows and cabins probably began the series of events that led to the Pinhook massacre. But not all of the Indians who participated in the hostilities were fugitives of the "Meeker Massacre," as the Ute reservation uprising was quickly dubbed. The group of renegade troublemakers is said to have been a mixed bag of Utes and Paiutes.

The trouble began in May 1881, when a band of Indians raided ranches near Dolores, Colorado. The Indians killed three ranchers and got away with a large number of horses, nine hundred pounds of flour,

Portrait of a proud Ute warrior
from the canyons of eastern Utah

an estimated $1,000 in paper currency, some guns, and seventy-five pounds of ammunition. The trail of the natives went west toward Utah. It took a few days to organize a posse and the Indians got a good head start.

The band of renegades traveled to Butler Wash, near the Mormon town of Bluff, Utah, where they stole more horses and shot at a local rancher. The next day, a brave and unsuspecting group of eight or nine Mormon stockmen rode right into the Indian camp and took their horses back without a fight. The Indians admired courage and were likely impressed by the audacity of the ranchers.

It was some days later before the ranchers learned of the killings and thefts in Colorado. The "boys from Bluff" reported that there were about thirty adult male Indians and about sixty women and children in the Indian camp. They said the natives were well armed and had about 150 horses, a big wad of paper money, and a herd of sheep and goats.

After surrendering fifteen of their stolen horses to the brave boys from Bluff, the Indians headed north toward the Blue Mountains, stealing hundreds of horses and shooting hundreds of domestic cattle along the way. When they raided the Double Cabin Ranch of "Spud" Hudson near Monticello, Hudson organized a twelve-man posse of local ranchers to pursue and punish the culprits. However, after cutting the trail and realizing the large number of Indians he was chasing, Hudson went back to the settlements and doubled the size of his posse. He then prudently followed the slow-traveling, sheep-herding, renegade rascals for a few weeks at a respectable distance. The posse could have confronted the renegades, "but feared pressing the chase because of possible ambush in the canyons." Old Spud Hudson was not a fool.

At the same time, a posse of about sixty-five men was on the way from Colorado. The Colorado posse was led by "Captain" Bill Dawson and Billy May, a brother of one of the slain Colorado ranchers. The Colorado posse was actually two posses combined. Men from some towns swore allegiance to Dawson, while men from other towns swore allegiance to May. This split in loyalties and command structure would later prove to be a detriment on the eve of the battle. The army also sent troops, but they got to the battle site way too late to do anything but help clean up the mess. Eastern Utah's biggest Indian fight was a true cowboy-and-Indian affair.

The Utah and Colorado posses joined forces near the Blue Mountains. The Indian trail was headed north and the Colorado men went on in hot pursuit, eager for a fight. The Utah posse had been shadowing the hostiles for almost three weeks by then and they were very cautious, tired, and saddle sore, and their horses had sore feet. They followed along behind the Colorado posse at a much slower pace.

As is the case in most human events where blood is spilled and emotions run high, there is a good deal of confusion as to what exactly took place over the next few days. Eyewitness accounts vary, numbers don't add up, and some posse members surely wanted to sanitize the record after suffering a humiliating defeat. The story is also complicated by lies, myth, and folklore, and some accounts were surely embellished with the passing of the years.

It is known that there were signs in the sky on the eve of the battle. On the night of June 12, as the Colorado posse closed the gap on their quarry, a total lunar eclipse occurred. The Indians took it as a bad omen. And then, the very next night, there was a bright comet in the sky. The Indians told white men later that the signs in the heavens discouraged them and took the fight out of them. They said the Great Spirit was angry when he "darkened the moon and burned up a star." They said that if the white men had been willing to talk and not fight, the Indians might have given up the captured livestock and maybe even turned over the men who had killed the ranchers.

Some members of the posse, knowing Indian superstitions, suggested that they try to negotiate with the renegades using the comet and lunar eclipse as leverage in the bargaining. But sadly, other posse members were confident in their numbers and they wanted blood. They scoffed at any attempt to try to negotiate.

A serious rift developed among posse members as to tactics and leadership. The men were civilian volunteers and not under military discipline. They didn't have to follow blindly. Finally, in disgust, "Captain" Dawson told those who continued to question his judgment, "Boys! Strike [leave] for your country and your homes." Obligingly, about half of the posse members turned back to Colorado. It is difficult to reconcile the numbers as given in all accounts, but it is generally agreed that Dawson had about thirty-five men in the field when the fight started.

In the early morning of June 15, the posse attacked the Indians as they were in camp on Pack Creek, about eighteen miles south of Moab. Posse members said the Indians had about fifteen hundred stolen horses at that time and a herd of about eight hundred sheep and goats. The white men captured a sizeable number of horses, along with nine Indian women who were herding the horses. There was a quick, long-range gunfight, but no one was injured or killed. The Indians made off up the canyon, still herding a good portion of their stolen horses.

Dawson left thirteen men to guard the captured horses and women, and with the remainder of his force, he went on in hot pursuit. It seems incredible from this vantage point that he would have divided his force in such a way, but he did. His actions show contempt for the perceived fighting abilities of the natives. General Custer had made the same mistake only five years earlier at the battle of the Little Big Horn.

And so, in a story known only through an account from a man named Albert Rogers, the men left to guard the captives were soon preoccupied "playing cards" with the younger Indian women. While the cowboys were thus distracted, the older women made a break, jumping on horses and driving off the entire horse herd. The thirteen humiliated "guards" had to walk eighteen miles into Moab carrying their saddles over their shoulders.

However it happened, the loss of another thirteen men was a serious setback to Dawson's posse as he closed with the Indians. He had left Colorado with sixty-five well-armed men, but by the time he got into handgun range, he was down to about eighteen lonesome cowboys. The signs in the sky turned out to be a bad omen for the white guys.

The Indians fought a rear guard action while herding their stolen stock in front of them as they tried to get away. The posse and the Indians traded bullets, but kept a respectable distance between them until the Indians dropped into Pinhook Draw, a narrow chute of a canyon at the head of Castle Valley, with steep mountains on three sides and a bottom covered with oak bushes and juniper. Everyone could see that it was a great place for an ambush, and when the Indians disappeared into the Pinhook, Dawson feared just that. But he was hot on the trail and had the hostiles on the run. Prudently, he sent only six of his men forward into the trap, assuring them that he would be close behind with the rest of the force to come to the rescue.

Predictably, the advance party was ambushed and shot up pretty good. The Indians were well armed with repeating rifles, and they knew how to use them. As promised, Dawson came forward with the rest of his men, but a hail of gunfire pinned them down. The posse members said later that they estimated the band of Indians to consist of about sixty-five warriors with thirty-five women and children. This is the exact opposite of what the men from Bluff reported when they actually rode into the Indian camp and counted thirty men with about sixty women and children. Like General Custer, the cowboys saw a whole lot of Indians out there. And in reality, it is possible that the hostiles had recruited more warriors as they pillaged the Blue Mountain ranges.

The fight lasted for the rest of that day and

the Indians were extremely aggressive in the Pinhook fight. One renegade threw caution to the wind and jumped atop a large boulder to direct the efforts of the natives. While on top of the rock and fully exposed to cowboy gunfire, the Indian thumped his chest and yelled, in pretty good English, "Shoot, you cowardly sons-of-bitches." The posse members did shoot, but no one could hit the man.

The cowboys couldn't believe the brave man was an Indian, and at least one newspaper of the time reported him to be a Mexican outlaw in league with the renegades. Sadly, the Indians never revealed the brave warrior's name. Even years after the fight, there might have been repercussions for an Indian bold enough to taunt brave posse members hiding behind rocks.

into a second day before the Indians pulled out and escaped down Castle Valley to the Colorado River, where they turned east. Within a few days, they had slipped back into the relative safety of the Ute reservation in Colorado.

Reinforcements arrived too late to help the posse members. Eight were killed and three others seriously wounded. Two cowboys from Moab were killed as well. The poor guys were drawn to the sound of

The cowboy cemetery and monument at the site of the
Pinhook "Massacre" of 1881. The Pinhook fight was the largest single battle
ever fought between whites and Native Americans in the Moab area.
The fight left ten whites and an unknown number of Utes and Paiutes dead.
By all accounts, the Indians won. (author photo)

gunfire and came riding up to see what was happening. Unknowingly, they rode right into the Indian camp.

It was estimated that twenty-four Indians might have been killed during the battle, even though only two bodies were found at the site—one of them a woman. Faun McConkie Tanner (*The Far Country*) lists the number of Indian bodies found as seven—one of them a woman. An old Paiute named Mancos Jim, who had participated in the battle, told interviewers a few years later that twenty-two Indians had been killed.

However, it does seem unlikely that the Indians would have continued the fight while suffering casualties in the twenty-plus range. They were the aggressors in the battle and could leave at any time. If

The gravestone of those massacred at the Pinhook "Massacre" site
(author photo)

warrior numbers were close to thirty, as the boys from Bluff maintained, it is most likely they would have fled the fight before suffering 80-percent casualties. Mancos Jim was probably telling white interviewers what they wanted to hear.

Although the army followed the Indians back to their reservation, and some of the participants of the Pinhook fight were later identified, no Indian was ever hanged for the "Pinhook massacre," much to the disappointment of some of the whites. And it was said that some of the natives, in later years, took pride in having fought and won the battle.

Eight of the cowboys are still buried on the battlefield. Two others were transferred to graveyards in Colorado. In 1940 the Moab Lions Club dedicated a monument at the gravesite. The monument and the site of the Pinhook "Massacre" can be found just two miles off the La Sal Loop Road at the head of Castle Valley. It's a great place to visit on a quiet afternoon. If you stand very still and listen carefully, you can still hear the faint echo of gunfire down the valley.

Outlaws and In-Laws

The canyon country around Moab has always been a great place to get lost—unintentionally or deliberately. The quiet isolation of the area has attracted many types of special characters over the years, and motives for seeking the emptiness of the canyons have been varied. In modern times, many a slave of technology has dreamed of breaking the chains of corporate conformity to escape into the depths of the canyon country. It's what vacations to Moab are all about.

In the early days, the solitude of the canyons attracted outlaws as well as prospectors, ranchers, homesteaders, and hermits. There were places where the long arm of the law couldn't reach. It was a brave lawman who ventured into the canyons of the Colorado to track down a fugitive. A large desert area west of Moab is still known as the "Robber's Roost."

The 1870s began the era of famous outlaws and gunfighters of the American West. It was a time of rapid westward expansion and social upheaval following the American Civil War. Many of the most notorious outlaws were wandering ex-soldiers, uprooted and lost after the grand adventure that had been the War Between the States. Unable to adapt to the relative boredom of civilian life, some of the restless war veterans turned to banditry for excitement, fun, and profit.

Beginning in the 1880s and continuing into the 1920s, the list of outlaws known to have walked the streets of Moab reads like a who's who list from a Rogue's Gallery. Butch Cassidy and Sundance (Harry Longabaugh) were there, of course, as was Matt Warner, Tom Roach, Mont Butler, Bert Madden, Al Akens, Flat Nose George Curry, Harvey Logan, "Kid" Jackson, and the McCarty brothers, to name only a few. Moab was a crossroads on the outlaw trail for many years.

Tom Roach is not well known in the pages of outlaw literature, but he was probably Moab's worst bad man. Roach was one of the Blue Mountain cowboys who came from Texas in the 1880s to work for the Carlisle Cattle Company. He is known to have killed two men and a woman in the area, and was never brought to justice.

In 1888 Tom Roach killed a man called Injun Joe. Injun Joe was a real Indian who had been raised by a white family, but he was notoriously bad tempered. Witnesses said Injun Joe called old Tom Roach out, not expecting to lose the fight, but when the smoke had cleared, it was Injun Joe who bit the dust. Tom Roach was a true Pistolero. The community let the shooting slide as an issue of self-defense. Some might have been happy to be rid of bad-tempered Injun Joe.

And then, one fateful night, Tom Roach rode into the little town of Monticello to attend a dance. He had a bottle of booze in his saddlebag. The community dance hall was so small that only part of the crowd could get on the floor at any one time, so participants were given numbers. People with even numbers danced for a time, and then odd-numbered people got their chance to take the floor. Every few dances, a "floor manager" called out the change of numbers, and everyone would switch.

While he was waiting to dance, Tom Roach and some friends retired to the booze bottle in the saddlebag. It didn't take long for Roach to get roaring drunk. Upon returning to the dance hall, Roach found that he had missed his turn to dance. He became angry and pushed his way onto the dance floor. The floor manager intervened, telling him to wait his turn. Roach pulled a gun and threatened to kill the man. He then threatened the whole crowd, vowing to shoot anyone who tried to leave the dance.

Roach's good friend Joe McCord tried to talk him out of it. Roach growled that he'd shoot McCord, too. Betting his life on their friendship, McCord walked over to Roach and was promptly shot dead. Someone else produced a gun, and more shots were fired. Roach beat a hasty retreat out the back, jumped on his horse, and disappeared into the night. When the smoke cleared, a middle-aged woman, Mrs. Jane Walton, lay dead on the dancehall floor, a bullet through her heart. It was not known for sure if it was Tom Roach's bullet that struck down Mrs. Walton, but there were plenty of witnesses to who caused the incident, and everyone saw Roach shoot his friend McCord.

Incredibly, Roach was never brought to justice for either killing. He was never arrested, even though he is said to have openly visited friends in Moab after the incident. It is surprising that no citizens' posse was ever organized to run old Tom Roach down or chase him out of the territory. Roach must have been a pretty scary character— or he had a lot of friends in eastern Utah.

Moab's most famous outlaw gang was the McCarty brothers, sometimes known as The Blue Mountain Gang. The boys were actually from the nearby settlement of La Sal. The McCarty family had been one of the first ranching families in the area, staking a claim to a few thousands of acres in the shadow of the La Sal Mountains in 1877. The family patriarch, known as Doc McCarty, was a displaced Confederate Army surgeon from Tennessee.

The family worked hard and put together a fine ranch. And then, in 1885, they sold the ranch and holdings to the Pittsburgh Cattle Company for the ungodly sum of $35,000. With the money, Doc McCarty moved to the Pacific Northwest with his wife and four daughters, but his sons—Tom, George, and Bill—stayed in the area.

The boys were all young men, and seem to have lived happily on the proceeds of the ranch sale for a while. But some years later, Tom McCarty wrote that money and idle time had been his downfall. He began to hang around with unsavory characters and soon was addicted to gambling. Horse races were his weakness.

When his inheritance was all squandered at the racetrack, Tom McCarty turned back to what he knew best—the cattle business. Only this time he was too impatient to start at the bottom to build another ranch. Instead, he turned to rustling other men's livestock.

Stealing cows was a risky business in the days when all cowboys carried guns, and the rewards of rustling were meager to a man who was accustomed to having his pockets full of silver. It didn't take Tom McCarty long to turn to where the real money was—in the banks. His wayward ways were influenced by his brother-in-law, Matt Warner. Matt Warner was a famous outlaw in eastern Utah, and Tom McCarty was married to Matt's sister, Teenie.

Matt Warner was a good friend of Butch Cassidy, and for a time, Matt, Butch, and Tom McCarty were the three amigos. In 1889 they robbed a bank in Telluride, Colorado. Estimates of what they took range from $10,000 to $21,000. Either sum was a good haul in the days when lonesome cowboys worked for a dollar a day.

Butch Cassidy struck out on his own after the successful Telluride bank heist. It is said that he saw serious character flaws in his two bank-robbing partners that could get them all killed. Matt Warner was mean and quick to anger. Tom McCarty was reckless and impulsive. Butch Cassidy was a gentleman

after the Telluride robbery, the outlaws passed through Moab on their way to the Robber's Roost. They were flush with stolen loot, and when crossing the river on the ferryboat, headed north, Butch Cassidy smiled as he tipped the ferryman a shiny $20 gold piece. Of course, the official story said the outlaws had "commandeered" the ferry in making good their escape.

Robert LeRoy Parker, a.k.a. Butch Cassidy, southeastern Utah's
most famous outlaw. History says he was killed in Bolivia in 1908.
His family says he died an old man in Spokane in 1937.
(Photo courtesy of the Western Railroad and Mining Museum in Helper, Utah)

bandit. He charmed people. Butch was destined to become the most
famous outlaw in the intermountain West—and one of the most long-
lived. He eventually went on to organize his own gang called "The
Wild Bunch."

Butch was never known to have killed a man in his days of bank and train holdups. He seems to have been cool and calculated, and he had lots of friends. He was one of the best and luckiest outlaws to ever leave tracks in the dusty streets of Moab—and he was never brought to justice. The adventures of Butch Cassidy and his partner Harry Longabaugh (The Sundance Kid) have been dramatized in the movies and several books, and it was widely reported that the two desperados went to hell in a blaze of glory in a big gunfight with the Bolivian Army in 1908. But rumors persist that the real Butch Cassidy (Robert LeRoy Parker) came back from Bolivia and died peacefully in bed in Spokane, Washington, in 1937. His sister claimed that he lived there for many years under the assumed name of William Phillips.

In the meantime, Tom McCarty and his brothers, George and Bill, formed their own outlaw gang—at least as legend tells it—and became very adept at cattle rustling and stealing horses. However, it was bank robbing that finally plowed them under. With fond memories of making such a fine profit by robbing the Telluride bank in 1889, Tom decided to do it again.

In 1893, Tom and Bill McCarty robbed a bank in Delta, Colorado. Bill's teenaged son Frank went along as a junior partner. The outlaws were in a hurry to get the money and go, but an obstinate teller refused to open a cash drawer and then cried out for help. Tom McCarty shot the man, killing him instantly. Butch Cassidy was right about Tom McCarty—he was reckless and impulsive.

The shot from the bank alerted nearby shopkeepers, and the owner of a hardware store ran into the street with a rifle. As the three desperados mounted their horses and raced for the edge of town, the rifleman shopkeeper shot Bill McCarty from the saddle. When young Frank rode back to help his father, the shopkeeper got him, too. Both were killed. Tom McCarty got away and disappeared before the Colorado lawmen could run him down. Where he went and what happened to him, no one seems to know for sure. There are rumors that he ended up in Wyoming or Montana.

✖ ✖ ✖

Gunsmoke in the Canyon

As reported in the Grand Valley Times *in March 1899, Sheriff Jesse Tyler of Moab and a citizen posse were caught up in a Wild West shootout that would have made John Wayne proud—except that everyone involved was a lousy shot. It all began when petty criminals "Silvertip," "Blue John," and "Indian Ed" passed through town after a horse-stealing foray into Wyoming and Colorado. True to their nature, the outlaws helped themselves to a few horses and mules belonging to other people.*

Horse stealing was a hanging offense in the old West. Sheriff Tyler organized a posse of five men and tracked the rascals across the Green River and into the Robber's Roost. Losing the trail in the sand flats and tangle of canyons in the Roost, the lawmen went to Hanksville and then as far south as the Henry Mountains trying to find a guide to show them the trails in and out of the outlaw sanctuary. Residents of Hanksville seem to have had a perpetual truce with the outlaws, and the good sheriff got no takers.

But then, while traveling back toward the town of Green River, Sheriff Tyler and his men cut a fresh trail leaving the Roost and going west toward the San Rafael Swell. The lawmen followed and were able to locate the outlaw camp by watching for a campfire after dark. The sheriff and his posse were able to sneak up on the outlaws during the night, but could not approach the camp undetected, since the bad guys were camped in an overhanging rock shelter among the ledges.

The lawmen waited until morning, when a "half-breed Indian" left the camp for his nature call. As the outlaw took care of business, he was ordered to throw his hands in the air and surrender. Instead, he went for his gun. A quick gunfight erupted and the Indian was badly wounded. He was last seen "crawling away behind some rocks." The posse had the outlaws pinned down in their wilderness camp, but the bad guys had lots of ammunition, and they fought like tigers.

The lawmen shot at the outlaws, and the outlaws shot at the lawmen. The air was filled with lead and the canyon with smoke as the echo of →

73

the gunfight drifted out over the sand flats of the Robber's Roost. The altercation went on for more than two hours, with bullets zipping through the air and pinging off the rocks. Bushes, trees, sandbumps, and blue sky were shot full of holes. Later, the lawmen sheepishly admitted that more than two hundred rounds had been fired with no casualties on either side—other than the Indian caught with his pants down.

Finally, with the fighting spirit and ammunition of the posse all used up, the sheriff decided it was time to go home. The outlaws were left in possession of the battlefield with their freedom and reputations intact. Score one for the bad guys.

The lawmen rounded up a small herd of nearby horses and mules to take back to Moab. Unfortunately, to add insult to injury, once back in Moab, Sheriff Tyler was promptly sued by a Mrs. Jack Moore, who said that two of the horses were hers and the sheriff had taken them illegally. It was not a good day for the good sheriff.

If the case went to trial, it was never reported in the paper. Sheriff Tyler was killed in another shootout with outlaws on the Book Cliffs just a few months later. Being a frontier lawman was a tough job.

And Just Who Was This Matt Warner?

†

Matt Warner, Tom McCarty's brother-in-law, was born in 1864 as Willard Erastus Christiansen in the little town of Ephraim, Utah. He was the son of a Mormon Bishop and the Bishop's fifth polygamist wife. Willard fled his hometown while still a teenager when he thought he had killed another boy in a fight over a girl. He had pounded the other boy's head with a rock.

Down and out with nowhere to go, the wayward kid eventually hooked up with a band of cattle rustlers in Brown's Hole, on the Green River south of Rock Springs, Wyoming. Believing that he was wanted for murder, Willard assumed the name Matt Warner to throw the lawmen off his trail. Incredibly, he would learn some years later that he didn't kill the other boy and no one was looking for him.

Matt Warner became good at cattle rustling, and he swaggered a little among the outlaws in his assumed role as a wanted man killer. And being more resourceful than most frontier outlaws, Warner used some of his stolen livestock to start a ranch in the Diamond Mountain area near Vernal, Utah. But only a few years later, when the law started closing in on his rustling headquarters at the Diamond Mountain Ranch, Warner fled south to Arizona. There, needing money, he robbed a bank in St. Johns, Arizona, making off with about $900. The good citizens of Arizona were outraged and chased him all the way back to the Robber's Roost in eastern Utah. At the Robber's Roost, Warner was able to escape the Arizona posse and lay low for a while.

It was not long after the Arizona incident that Warner hooked up with his brother-in-law, Tom McCarty, and his friend, Butch Cassidy, to do the famous bank job in Telluride. Splitting with Cassidy shortly after the Telluride bank heist, Matt Warner hid out in Star Valley, Wyoming, for about a year. While there, he married a fourteen-year-old girl named Rosa Rumel, who died only a few years later of cancer. Shortly before her death, Rosa gave birth to a baby boy, who was given away to a good family (Warner was in prison at the time). The baby died while still a child.

In 1896, Warner went to work as a hired gun for a mining firm seeking protection from claim-jumpers. Unfortunately, he and another gunslinger named Bill Wall were a little too eager in their role as company enforcers. In a confrontation with three suspicious characters, they killed two of the men and badly wounded the third. The company gunslingers were promptly arrested and tried for murder. There was no evidence that the three men were anything but legitimate prospectors.

It is said that Matt Warner used a large stash of buried bank robbery loot to pay for his legal defense, and maybe even to grease the wheels of justice with a few well-placed bribes. Warner escaped a hangman's noose and went to the Utah State Prison in September 1896, but was released in January 1900 after serving only three years and three months for a double murder.

After paying his debt to society, Warner turned from his outlaw ways and moved to Price, Utah, where he lived for many years, marrying a second wife and fathering three children. He was elected justice of the peace and served as a deputy sheriff for many years. Small town America was a very practical place in those days. Sometimes the best lawman was an ex-outlaw with a reputation for being a tough character.

Matt Warner ran for sheriff of Carbon County in 1912, and probably would have been elected had he used his old outlaw name. Everyone knew Matt Warner, but he was listed on the ballot by his

Willard Erastus Christiansen, a.k.a. the outlaw Matt Warner.
After a distinguished career as a cattle rustler and a bank robber,
Matt Warner went to the Utah State prison for a double murder.
Paroled after only three years for "good behavior" and a possible bribe or two,
he gave up the outlaw life and served as Justice of the Peace
and a deputy sheriff in Price, Utah. This photo was taken about 1920,
during his days as a respectable lawman.
(Photo courtesy of the Western Railroad and Mining Museum in Helper, Utah)

real name, Willard Christiansen. Few people recognized that name, and Warner didn't get enough votes to win.

Matt Warner died in Price in 1938. It has been said that he drank himself to death after a popular book of the day, *The Outlaw Trail*, accused him of abusing his first wife, the teenaged Rosa Rumel. It was a charge that he angrily denied as he sank deeper and deeper into the whiskey bottle. He died at the age of 74, one of the last of the old-time outlaws to meet the Ghost Riders in the sky.

The era of frontier outlaws and lawmen lasted through the 1920s in Moab. In 1923 the Moab bank was robbed by three desperados who were chased out into the desert and captured by sheriff's deputies. And in 1929 a very popular Moab lawman, R.D. Westwood, was shot and killed when two petty thieves broke out of jail.

Westwood's killers—one hiding in the hills south of town and the other riding a cottonwood log down the river trying to escape—were quickly apprehended. The men were tried, convicted, and sent to the Utah State Penitentiary for life. The old West was becoming tame. Had it happened thirty years earlier, the good citizens of Moab might have hanged the killers on the steps of the county courthouse.

Richard Westwood was the third old-time lawman to give his life in defense of the community. In 1900 Deputy Sheriff Westwood had taken over as acting Grand County sheriff after outlaws in the Book Cliffs had killed Sheriff Jesse Tyler and Deputy Sam Jenkins. He was still serving as a deputy sheriff at the time of his murder nearly thirty years later. Westwood was sixty-six years old when he was ambushed and killed by the two escapees. His death marked the end of an era.

✠ ✠ ✠

The Ghost Wolf

There is a legend in southeastern Utah about a great phantom wolf who stalked the mountains and desert glens of the Land of Moab. The wolf was

only a shadow in the timber, but his tracks and handiwork haunted ranchers for years. The ghost wolf was known as Bigfoot or Three Toes. Ranchers said his tracks were four inches across and the right-front paw was missing a toe. The wolf had chewed the toe off to escape a trap.

Though sheep became the primary targets of wolves as herds of elk and deer diminished, stockmen estimated that wolves killed more than 650 cattle in the Utah–Colorado border area between 1910 and 1920. Bigfoot and his pack were credited with most of the kills. It was said the wolves often killed for sport, dragging down several cows in a single night and eating only parts of each animal.

Bigfoot was so hated and feared by the cowboys that the bounty for his hide reached $1,000 dollars by 1920. Professional trappers from as far away as Mexico and Canada came to Moab to try to catch the phantom. A couple of Paiute Indian trappers came back to town with stories that the phantom wolf had supernatural powers. More than one trapper stayed on the ghost wolf's trail for more than a year without ever spotting the animal. Bigfoot blended into the shadows and seemed to vanish at will, and after months of having the ghost wolf evade every trapping effort, at least one old-timer swore that Bigfoot was possessed by the devil. ➙

But then, a 1920 edition of the Grand Valley Times *ran the follow-ing article:*

> Old Big Foot, known as the Peavine Wolf and the Outlaw, which during the past several years has inflicted so much damage to stock-men in San Juan County, has at last been captured and the pelt delivered to the San Juan Commissioners for bounty. In addition to the bounty offered by the state, there has been a standing offer by stockmen of a reward of a thousand dollars for the capture of Big Foot. The animal was captured last week by Roy Mussleman, a trap-per on the south side of Elk Mountains in San Juan County. The pelt measured eight feet from tip to tip. The wolf is supposed to be twelve years old, as his fur is light and when seen from a distance appeared almost white. Big Foot has ranged a circle of some 100 miles, accord-ing to stockmen. He was followed by a pack of coyotes who lived off the carcasses the wolf left. Cowmen and Indians in the region which span the range said that his hoarse howl could be heard a distance of five miles. During his ravages among the livestock he has slaughtered thousands of dollars worth of cattle, horses, and sheep.

The ghost wolf was finally dead, but old Bigfoot might have had supernat-ural powers after all, for he seems to have come back at least one more time. Instead of selling the hide, Roy Mussleman hung the pelt inside a barn in Monticello as a trophy of his trapping skills. The barn caught fire and burned to the ground. The last earthly remains of the phantom wolf entered the air as smoke and scattered through the canyons and the Blue Mountain ranges.

Some say old Bigfoot is still out there. The ghost wolf watches from the shadows, and sometimes, when the wind blows in eastern Utah, people swear they hear more than wind howling in the canyons.

✠ ✠ ✠

The Killing of Flat Nose George

S hortly after the turn of the twentieth century, a minor bad guy named Tom Dilly started a fight in the little town of Castle Dale, Utah. The incident produced a warrant for Dilly's arrest. Not eager to face the charges, the bad-news boxer fled to the Robber's Roost.

A few months later, in April 1900, a foreman for the Webster Cattle Company rode up on a man altering the brand on one of the company's calves not far from the town of Green River, just north of the Robber's Roost. Prudently, the cowboy range boss turned his back and rode away, choosing to notify authorities rather than risk his life in a gunfight on the open range. From the description given by the cattle foreman, and because of recent events, everyone assumed the rustler was Tom Dilly.

Two county sheriffs, Jesse Tyler of Moab and William Preece from Vernal, met in Green River to investigate the incident. After consulting with the range boss, the lawmen set out to bring the bad guy to justice. They pointed their horses into the badlands, split up to cover more ground, and began making large sweeps over hill and dell looking for tracks. It wasn't long before Sheriff Preece cut the outlaw's trail, and within a short distance, he overtook the bad guy. A six-mile running gunfight followed, with the outlaw escaping across the Green

River, where he holed up in some large boulders. Sheriff Preece kept him pinned down with rifle fire, but couldn't get across the river to apprehend the man.

Alerted by the sound of the gunfight, Sheriff Tyler rode to the scene and was able to assess the situation, cross the river unseen, and approach the outlaw from the same side of the river. Apparently not knowing that he was surrounded and facing multiple lawmen, the rustler exposed too much of himself to Sheriff Tyler and was shot dead.

The two lawmen were surprised to discover that the very dead outlaw was not Tom Dilly after all, but a more famous and more dangerous outlaw, Flat Nose George Curry. George Curry was the owner of a prominent proboscis, and his outlaw name had originally been Big Nose George—until he objected. So with a little tongue-in-cheek humor, the irreverent outlaws had started calling him Flat Nose George, usually behind his back. The name stuck, and he was Flat Nose George Curry ever after.

Flat Nose George was a member of the Hole-in-the-Wall Gang from up near Brown's Park by the Wyoming border. He was wanted for bank and train robbery as well as cattle rustling. Even though they got the wrong guy, it was a fine catch for the two law officers. Score one for the good guys.

Unfortunately, Flat Nose George had a few friends. One of them was Harvey Logan, also known as "Kid Curry." When Harvey Logan came from Texas as a young man and joined the Hole-in-the-Wall Gang, Flat Nose George had become his mentor. Logan was so taken with the big-nosed outlaw that he adopted the man's last name, becoming Kid Curry in honor of his friend. Kid Curry was very upset when he leaned that his father figure had been killed by Sheriff Tyler of Moab. He vowed to take revenge.

Only about a month after the killing of Flat Nose George, Sheriff Tyler was on the trail of Tom Dilly again. Tyler wanted Dilly bad. The petty outlaw had pulled a gun on one of the sheriff's deputies, Sam Jenkins, to escape arrest, and Tyler wanted the rascal to pay for his insolence.

In May 1900, Tyler got word that Dilly was holed up near Hill Creek, in the Book Cliffs, several miles north of the little town of Thompson Springs. He took two of his deputies on the search: Sam Jenkins, who had a personal score to settle, and Herbert Day. Some accounts say that a young boy, Mert Wade, accompanied the lawmen, too, probably as a camp tender. Again, Sheriff Tyler linked up with Uintah County sheriff Preece, who led a posse of four men from Vernal.

The lawmen had been out for about three weeks when Sheriff Tyler spotted what he thought was an Indian camp in some willows. Because the camp was in a sheltered place, it was difficult to see for sure who and how many were there. The sheriff and his deputies went to investigate. Sheriff Preece and his men were a few miles away searching another area.

The three lawmen dismounted a short distance from the camp, and Sheriff Tyler and Deputy Jenkins approached on foot. Deputy Day remained behind, holding the horses. As the two men walked toward the camp, Day said they announced their approach, hollering something like, "Hello, boys, we are entering your camp."

It was a fatal mistake. The two lawmen walked right into a nest of outlaws. Quickly realizing their mistake, Sheriff Tyler and Deputy Jenkins both turned to run. They were cut down by a hail of gunfire, both shot in the back. The bad guys shot at Deputy Day, but he was further away with the horses and was able to escape unharmed. The deputy beat a hasty retreat, running to find Sheriff Preece and his posse, leaving the bodies of his two companions in the dirt. The surviving deputy said later that he estimated about twenty horses were in the camp.

When Day rode up wild-eyed on a lathered horse to tell the tale of the large outlaw camp and the two dead officers, Sheriff Preece thought it most advantageous to quit the field of battle and send for reinforcements. The men from Vernal and the surviving Moab deputy went south, off the Book Cliffs, to Thompson Springs, about thirty-five miles north of Moab. The telegraph was soon humming with news of the killings.

Predictably, the whole state of Utah was outraged by the killing of the law officers. Posses were formed in Moab, Vernal, and Price to hunt the outlaws down. Governor Wells even sent a posse of Utah State law officers to Green River by way of the railroad to assist in any way they could.

The combined posses recovered the bodies of Tyler and Jenkins and then combed the Book Cliffs for weeks searching for the outlaws—who weren't there anymore, of course. Posse members went clear into Wyoming tracking leads, but no one was ever arrested or charged with the killing of the two law officers.

Kid Curry was happy to take credit for the murders of Sheriff Tyler and Deputy Jenkins, but it was never proven that he was the shooter or that he was even in the outlaw camp. He had promised revenge for the killing of Flat Nose George, and maybe he got it. Who knows?

As Kid Curry, Harvey Logan took Flat Nose George Curry's name on to other outlaw adventures until he was finally plowed under in a shootout with lawmen near Rifle, Colorado, in June 1904. The twentieth century was hard on the old outlaw bands. Modern technology was proving deadly, and an era of rapid communications, greater mobility, and increasing population was shrinking the old outlaw haunts. Even the Robber's Roost wasn't impenetrable anymore. The wild and romantic days of the old West were nearly done.

⚡ ⚡ ⚡

The Dubinky Ghost

There is a great story about a couple of brothers, Red and Dubinky Anderson, who hauled freight along Highway 191 through Moab in the early decades of the twentieth century.

While on the road one fateful evening, the brothers decided to stop and camp amid the ruins of Valley City, about six miles south of Crescent

Junction. Valley City is one of eastern Utah's many ghost towns, and a few old foundations and the ruins of a cellar can still be seen from the highway today. The brothers had heard tales that an old, abandoned, two-storied hotel at the site was haunted, but to prove to each other that they were brave young men, they decided to stay in the old building anyway. We can imagine them teasing, giggling, and telling spooky stories as they rolled out their bedrolls for the night.

The sun went down, the stars came out, and crickets sang in the darkness. The boys snuggled into their camp quilts, tired after a long day on the road. And then, later in the night, one of them heard the creak of a board and peeked out of his blankets to see the hazy shadow of a woman slowly descending the stairs in the moonlight.

Next came pandemonium. Shouts, screams, and the trample of feet echoed across the desert. Blankets and heels flew through the air as the boys broke from the building and scattered into the night. Red went north and Dubinky went west, neither of them stopping for a long, long time. ⇢

Red made his way to Thompson Springs, about fifteen miles away, and recruited help to go back to look for his brother. When the search party arrived at the haunted house the next morning, they found a very distressed and frightened woman. Who she was, where she came from, and where she was going is not known, but she, too, had been camping in the old hotel when the brothers stopped for the night. Being afraid, she had hidden on the second floor of the building, where she was trapped when the unsuspecting brothers put their bedrolls in the foyer. She had waited until late at night and then tried to sneak away while the boys were sleeping.

The rescue party tracked Dubinky Anderson for ten miles over slick-rock, sage, and sand. He had traveled barefoot in the dark and made his way to a cowboy cabin in an area known today as Dubinky Wash and Dubinky Well, about ten miles west of Canyonlands Airport. Old timers in Moab don't remember if Dubinky Well and Dubinky Wash were named after Dubinky Anderson or if Anderson was nicknamed "Dubinky" because it was his place of refuge from the ghost. Either way, he must have had a tough time living down his reputation as a Ghostbuster.

Bank Bandit Follies

In 1923 the bank in Moab was robbed—well, sort of. When the dust had settled, the bank actually made thirty dollars on the deal. Sound incredible? It surely was. Jay Leno couldn't have written a better comedy script.

It all started when three bad guys decided to bust the Moab bank the old fashioned way—by being burglars. In the early morning hours of Friday, April 27, they began to saw through the bars on a back window of the bank. The hacksaw blade broke and they didn't have a spare. Not to be deterred, they pried open the front door using a wrecking bar.

Once inside the bank, the intrepid trio was figuring out how to get into the vault when the bank's bookkeeper just happened to pass by at two or three o'clock in the morning. Mr. Green saw the door to the bank ajar and dutifully stopped to investigate. He was promptly taken captive at gunpoint. He was gagged, tied up, and put in a coal shed under the watchful eye of one of the burglars.

The other two bad guys blew the door to the vault with nitroglycerin. They then set an explosive charge against the door of the safe and touched it off. Nothing. A second, larger charge did the trick, but destroyed the inside of the vault. A whole lot of paper money in the safe was also blown to smithereens, floating down over the crime scene like confetti. Incredibly, the sleepy little town slept through all three explosions. No one called the sheriff or went to see what the commotion was all about.

The burglars gathered up the greenback confetti and got away with about $7,000 in coins and paper currency. They stuffed the bookkeeper, bound and gagged, into the smoke-filled vault and told him they would leave the door open a crack so he didn't suffocate. Nice guys. They then gathered up their loot and headed for the hills.

But the bad-news bandits had tied the bookkeeper's feet without removing his cowboy boots. Once they were gone, the bookkeeper simply slipped out of his boots and walked down the street, barefoot and still tied up, to a neighbor's house, where he was able to sound the alarm—after someone removed his gag.

The next part is almost too silly to be true, but the fugitives made their escape on foot. Either they had no escape plan or something went terribly wrong. Some have speculated that the multiple explosions from inside the bank might have caused the getaway driver to flee. However it happened, the desperados didn't have a horse or an automobile and they didn't attempt to steal any. They simply lugged some heavy sacks of silver coins all the way to the north end of the river bridge and then hid in the rocks above Courthouse Wash. From their vantage point in the ledges, they spent the day watching the townspeople scurry about, spreading the news of the big bank heist.

When it got dark, they tried to sneak away, but not knowing the area, they got lost in the tangle of canyons and made little progress.

Sometime during that second night, the bad guys made the mistake of crossing the Moab–Thompson road. Their tracks in the sand were noticed the next morning by sheriff's deputies, who followed the trail far enough to find a tattered scrap of a $5 bill and the wrapper from a roll of coins. Knowing the doomed desperados wouldn't get far headed out into the desert on foot, the deputies went back to the nearby Courthouse Stage Station, had a good meal, borrowed another rifle, and then went back to track the rascals down.

The deputies caught the bad guys hiding in some sand dunes, and a couple of well-placed warning shots convinced them to surrender. The deputies also recovered three big rolls of tattered bills and three pistols the outlaws had buried in the sand. The bandits were then marched back to the road and taken to Moab.

In a plea deal, one of the bungling burglars agreed to lead the lawmen back to where the rest of the loot had been stashed. He took them to the north side of the river bridge and showed them where two bags of silver coins were hidden in a crack in the rocks and covered with dirt. When all of the stolen loot was counted and the tattered bills taped back together, it was determined that the bank had $30 more than was stolen. The burglars said the extra money belonged to them. What happened to the thirty bucks is not told in the literature, but one can guess that it probably went toward restitution for damages to the bank building.

A Town is Born

From the 1880s into the early years of the twentieth century, Moab was a rough-and-tumble little frontier town. The streets were dirt, irrigation ditches flowed through the middle of town, and young cottonwood trees and Lombardy poplars lined the streets and roadways. Houses were a mix of log cabins, mud-brick

Moab in 1900, two years before the town was incorporated
(Museum of Moab photo CH-14)

small homes, and a few modern, Victorian-style, wood-framed buildings with gables and porches. Every house had outbuildings: barns, cellars, sheds, and crannies (latrines). And most houses had a vegetable garden in the yard instead of a lawn. Chicken coops, pigpens, and corrals for horses and milk cows were in the back of the lot, a little farther away from the house.

There was mud and

the local watering holes (saloons) and barbershops were the real social centers of most small towns on the frontier. Like Hopi kivas, they were men's clubs where women were excluded—at least "respectable" women. Many frontier saloons doubled as brothels. Every town seemed to have a few "soiled doves" who sold their charms to eager cowboys who came to town every month or so to get rid of their hard-earned money.

horse manure in the streets in the wintertime, and deep sand, dust, and horse manure in the streets in the summertime. The business district contained just a few whipsawed board buildings, some with false fronts. Main Street was only a block or two long and had the usual small town commercial enterprises of the day, which generally consisted of a general mercantile or two, a blacksmith shop, a livery stable, probably a rooming house of some kind, perhaps a bank, sometimes a doctor's office, usually a barbershop, and always two or three saloons.

Every respectable little town like Moab also had at least one church and a school. Sometimes the two were combined into the same building. The church/school usually doubled as a meetinghouse for town gatherings, a place for community social events like dances and weddings, and sometimes a temporary safe shelter for outlying homesteaders who fled to town during times of Indian troubles.

Cowboys often spent months on the desert working with livestock before having an opportunity to go to town to buy supplies and have a few days off. They usually brought a wad of accumulated back pay and were impatient to spend it. Like young men everywhere, the boys were out for a little fun. There are stories of horse races through the middle of town, shots fired at tin cans and stray dogs, fistfights, practical jokes, and hedonistic drunken revelry. Whiskey was cheap in the days before government regulation and heavy taxation.

There was a religious element in town, too, and that was the Mormons, even though Moab was one of the few frontier towns in Utah not settled by official LDS church-initiated decree. Most of the population of Utah was Mormon in the 1800s, and many of the earliest settlers of Moab and Spanish Valley were Mormons. The Church of Jesus Christ of Latter-day Saints is still influential in the Land of Moab, as it is in all of Utah. However, the Mormons do not have a majority in Moab or Grand County today. Primarily because of large numbers of "outsiders" brought in by the mining and tourist industries, the LDS church in Grand County claims about 30 percent of the population.

In 1890 Grand County was split from Emery County, and Moab became the county seat, even though the town was unincorporated and not yet an "official" town. There really wasn't another choice. Unincorporated Moab held most of the new county's population, and it was the political, economic, and social center of the whole region. Even today, Moab is the only "real" town in a rural county that covers thirty-seven hundred square miles.

Grand County was named after the Grand—later to become the Colorado—River that flowed past Moab. And like the river, Grand County was a wild and untamed place in the 1890s. Government and law enforcement were stretched very thin. And even though the town had all of the trappings of a proper municipality, it was not officially incorporated until December 30, 1902, twelve years after it became a county seat.

Part of the reason the town was incorporated in 1902 was to create a tax base to facilitate the hiring of a town marshal. Local cowboys came to town often to let off steam, and some of the good citizens feared for their safety and the reputation of the town as a proper, civilized community. A petition to encourage incorporation claimed that a town marshal would "bring public carousing to a halt." The county sheriff had operated out of Moab for several years, but he was often out chasing bad guys in the Robber's Roost or on the Book Cliffs when drunken cowboys danced on the bar and shot at the moon. The town needed a full-time law enforcement presence.

In January 1903, the first town ordinances became law. Fees and licenses for doing business in the community were set. A general business license was $10 per year, peddlers were assessed at $100 per year, and a liquor license would set a saloonkeeper back by $400 per year. The cost of booze was on the rise.

Wages for city employees were set at $10 per year for city trustees (city managers), $40 per year for a city treasurer, $100 per year for a city clerk, and the princely sum of $50 per month—$600 per year—for a town marshal. The good citizens were offering big bucks for quality law enforcement. It was the beginning of a new century, and the wild and wooly days of the old West were coming to an end. People were beginning to see Moab as a respectable and civilized place.

❖ ❖ ❖

When Bears Ran in Packs and Nobody Danced with Wolves

There are some great stories about bears, cougars, and wolves in the Moab area. Most originate from the late pioneer period when the country was still untamed and the lamb and the lion would never consider sharing a rug in front of the fire. The following are excerpts from old newspapers.

Emery County Progress, *July 27, 1901*
RK Kello and a party of surveyors while locating oil lands in the hills near Sunnyside were attacked by a large number of bears one night last week. The men had retired and the wild beasts pounced upon the tents

and tore the canvas to pieces. Amos E. Petersen was badly hurt in the fight with the bears. Later the bears attacked a herd of sheep, killing fifty.

— — —

Grand Valley Times, *March 31, 1911*

Chased by ten wolves for more than a mile through Cedar canyon in the mountains northwest of Fort Collins, Al Hinton of Grover had a narrow escape from death Monday. He stumbled into a little used road where a homesteader, who was passing in a wagon, saved the lives of both by throwing out a quarter of beef to the hungry pack. The men escaped behind the racing team while the wolves fought over the flesh.

— — —

Grand Valley Times, *January 3, 1913*

Grand Junction, Colo.—Sacrificing five horses to wolves in order to save his own life, Victor Corn, a cattleman, finally reached Grand Junction in safety Monday night. Corn walked over forty miles with his fifty-pound saddle on his back before he reached safety.

The Cattleman started from the range in Utah with five horses. His first night's camp was made thirty-five miles from Grand Junction. Corn

had no thought of wolves the first night, but when he arose in the morning he found that three of his horses had been killed and practically devoured by the animals. Frightened, he started on with the remaining two horses, with the wolves in pursuit. The fourth horse was killed when Corn camped for the second night. On the third night he built a big fire, hoping to save his one remaining horse, but when he arose in the morning the fire was still smoldering but his horse had been taken away. He followed marks of blood for half a mile and then found the remains of his last horse. Corn then started on the last leg of his journey, fighting wolves all the way. He walked thirty miles before arriving at Thompson Springs, carrying his saddle on his back.

— — —

The Times Independent, *October 26, 1922*

Hell's Canyon, located near the head of Pack Creek in the La Sal mountains, seems to be the habitat of a colony of bears, and while deer may be scarce in that section there is no dearth of members of the bruin family, according to Oscar Stewart and T. E. Lassiter, who returned Thursday from a hunting excursion to that country. Messrs. Stewart and Lassiter, while searching for buckskin [deer], met up with ten head of bear, and they succeeded in killing four of them. They report that Hell's canyon seemed to be full of bear and they could have shot more if their supply of ammunition had not given out.

The Real Effects
of Climate Change

G rand County, Utah, is more than three times the size of the state of Rhode Island, and yet there is only one town with a population of five thousand or more in the whole county. That town is Moab. It isn't that other towns haven't tried. Grand County is littered with ghost towns. A quick count finds at least twenty-one, and there may be even more.

Why so many ghost towns? There are several reasons, but the main one is a change in climate. The Land of Moab today is a much drier place than it was in the 1800s and the early 1900s. Global warming? Perhaps. But drier conditions are more likely due to a normal and natural shift in weather patterns that have affected the area over many thousands of years. The Anasazi were dry-farming most of San Juan County, just south of Moab, between eight hundred and fifteen hundred years ago, so we know the climate was much wetter back then. Also, several of the early pioneers reported flowing water and broad expanses of grassland where none is found today. The land has changed a great deal.

Most of the Grand County ghost towns were settled between 1880 and about 1920 by farmers and ranchers. A few were appendages of the railroad, one was a coalmine town, a few were hard-rock mining camps, and some served a combination of economic elements. Here are some of the more interesting ones:

Thompson Springs, about 35 miles north of Moab, was once a thriving railroad town. Settled originally as a ranch in the early 1880s, the place became an important water stop for the old steam engines of the D&RGW. There was a large stockyard there, too, and Thompson Springs became a regional transportation link for shipping livestock to the eastern markets. Passengers rode the rails in and out of Grand County from the little depot, and there was a good hotel and café there in the early years. A frontier saloon did a brisk business with the cowboys, sheep men, and railroaders. Even the California Zephyr made the town a regular stop from 1942 until 1970. But in the 1950s, railroad engines went to diesel-electric, and the new and improved interstate highway went past and not through the little community. Today a few people still call Thompson Springs home, but most of the town is in ruins, a relic of a rich and colorful past.

Valley City, about 15 miles southwest of Thompson Springs, was begun in 1905 as a commercial farming venture by the Grand Valley Land and Mineral Company of Indianapolis, Indiana. The partners expected to plant twenty-five hundred fruit tees and create a thriving community in the process. Shares in the venture were sold to several investors in the Midwest. Unfortunately, the enterprise went bust in 1908 when a flood took out the dirt reservoir. Some have suggested that the whole thing was only a scam to cheat investors. Ruins of a few buildings, including a two-story "hotel," sat vacant until 1919, when a family named Burdick purchased the land and began farming and ranching there. The Burdicks lived in Valley City until the mid-1930s, when dry conditions and poor markets forced them out. The "town" has been vacant ever since. Almost nothing remains.

Sego was a coal mining camp about five miles north of Thompson Springs. Thompson Canyon forks about 3.5 miles above the town, and the right-hand (east) fork is known as Sego Canyon. The old town site is another mile up the road. A coalmine was developed there in 1901 to supply coal for the railroad. At its heyday in the 1920s, the mine employed between 150 and 200 miners. The mine was closed in 1954 and the town died completely. Many of the best buildings were moved from the site or torn down.

The towns of Cisco and Westwater were both railroad towns. Like Thompson Springs, Westwater began as a ranch in the early 1880s and then became a railroad stop. Track crews and railroad employees were housed there into the 1930s. In the 1920s, Westwater and the surrounding area was home to about one hundred people. The place slowly reverted back to a ranch by the early 1950s. Cisco, too, was a water stop for steam locomotives. Cisco's main claim to fame is having been the home of Charlie Steen, the "Cisco Kid," who got rich during the Uranium Boom of the 1950s (more on him later). The town of Cisco was featured in the 1991 movie *Thelma and Louise.*

Danish Flats and Marrs were both agricultural communities out in the sand flats, where today nothing grows but tumbleweeds, bunchgrass, and cactus. If there was ever a testimonial as to how the country has changed in a hundred years, it is the fact that people once believed they could make a living dry farming those areas—and actually did for a few years.

Like Valley City, Marrs was the creation of a land development company—this one headquartered in Denver. The site was located on Cottonwood Wash, a little south and east of Cisco. At least twenty families took up land in Marrs beginning in 1910, and the little community existed with some struggles until about 1919, when the land development company went broke. Without the guiding hand and cooperative efforts made possible by the company, Marrs dried up and blew away. Actually, the last few families to live there considered themselves to be residents of nearby Cisco.

Danish Flats was north of the present interstate highway along Danish Wash, north of Cisco. A man named Quintas Cato was the first to homestead the area in 1916. By 1921 the area was said to contain some "highly productive" farms, and as many as fifty people had

This 1926 or 1927 Model-T Ford was part of Dale Parriott's
auto stage line along the Colorado River from Moab. This narrow spot in the
road was just past the ten-mile marker on River Road—State Highway 128.
(Museum of Moab photo RP-3)

filed for homesteads in the area. The "town" was really only a collection of farms spread over about three square miles. There was never a formal town center. The farmers dry-farmed the area and diverted some irrigation water from nearby Cottonwood Creek.

For a few years all went well at Danish Flats. And then it stopped raining. By 1928 even Cottonwood Wash was dry, and the last of the homesteaders had starved out and moved away. Today, looking out over the bleak sand flats of the area, it is amazing that it ever looked inviting enough to tempt people to try to farm there.

Castleton was a thriving mining and cowboy town in 1901 when the local folks filed for incorporation (a year before Moab did). Castleton was located about ten miles up Castle Valley, east of Moab. It is a beautiful setting, and the town prospered for a few years. The local economy was fueled by mining operations in the La Sal Mountain regions. Gold, silver, copper, lead, and even small amounts of uranium were mined at the turn of the last century. Cattle, sheep, and farming played an important role, too. But by the 1920s, the mines were playing out, the land was drying up, and people were moving away. By 1930 nearly everyone had gone.

There are many other ghost towns in the area. Each one has a special story and a unique history. Each one is a monument to human hopes and dreams, and each of those dreams has a name: Webster City, Elgin, Woodside, Richardson, Dewey, Mesa, Polar Mesa, Bachelor Basin, Miners Basin, Beaver Basin, Crystal Carbon, Yellow Cat, and Bueno (Poverty Flats).

The Earliest UFO Cover-Up?

1917 was the year America entered World War I. It was also a time when most people still used horses as their primary means of transportation. There were very few automobiles. Aircraft of that time were primitive machines, made of canvas and wood, with open cockpits and very limited range and capabilities—and there were no airplanes or landing strips anywhere in southern Utah, anyway. Those facts make Moab's first recorded UFO sighting all the more intriguing.

On the night of July 20, 1917, sawmill workers on the south side of the La Sal Mountains saw lights in the sky, an unheard of phenomenon in those days before satellites and jet airliners. The workers called their fellows to come and see, and several people witnessed the event. They described what they saw as "four airplanes, all equipped with strong searchlights." It was between ten and eleven at night, and "the machines did considerable maneuvering above the La Sal flats" and "were evidently signaling to each other."

Three of the flying machines came from the east and another joined them from the south. "One of the ships had a powerful light, and its signals consisted of a long, brilliant flash. The other machines answered with quick flashes. After hovering over La Sal for some time, the airplanes sailed southwest over Dry Valley and toward the junction of the Grand [Colorado] and Green Rivers."

The event caused "much excitement," according to the local newspaper, and by early August the lights in the sky had become a "nightly" occurrence. A special investigator for the Justice Department was sent, and his first conclusion was that the lights were "enemy" aircraft, because the army could not account for American aircraft being there. The nearest military airbase was in Columbus, New Mexico, over four hundred miles away and far beyond the range of the bi-wing Jennies of the day.

On August 8, the Grand Valley Times reported that the government investigator was calling for military aircraft to patrol the area and challenge the "enemy" airships. However, by August 17, the government man took a different stand and released the following statement: "Aeroplanes, which have been quite frequent in the southern part of the district during the past few weeks, need cause no further agitation or concern on our part or that of the general public." The newspaper said that the reports had all been investigated and "while he [the government agent] is not at liberty to divulge the circumstances surrounding the operation of these machines throughout this section, he assures us they are not enemy aircraft and their business is perfectly legitimate."

What the flying machines were, where they came from, and what prompted the final, reassuring conclusion, is still a mystery. In the years since, no information has been found to suggest that the army was doing any type of training in the area—especially training that involved flying machines with range and capabilities far beyond what was possible in 1917.

Moab:
Uranium Capital of the World

Sometime in the shadowy world of prehistory, American Indians around Moab discovered radioactive carnotite. Carnotite is a soft, yellow—and sometimes red—mineral that was ground into powder and used as body paint by the natives. Body paint was always in high demand among indigenous peoples, and the radioactive pigment was a "hot" item at tribal swap meets.

Later, and for several years, white men used the atomic mineral as a coloring agent in ceramics as well as paint. Varying shades of color could be made by altering formulas and adding other elements. There are still flowerpots and coffee mugs out there somewhere that glow in the dark and make Geiger counters sing.

In the 1890s, carnotite was scientifically analyzed and discovered to contain both uranium and vanadium. And by 1898, a Polish woman, born Maria Sklodowska but better known as the French physicist Madame Curie, discovered that the rare elements radium and polonium could be extracted from a black mineral called pitch-blende. In the early 1900s, the first small-scale uranium mines were opened on the Colorado Plateau to provide raw material to Madame Curie and other European scientists.

Beginning in the 1920s and lasting until after World War II, radioactive minerals were mined primarily for their vanadium content. Vanadium was found to be a great tempering agent in the making of steel. Vanadium ore was mined in the canyons around Moab, the Rico mining district in western Colorado, and the San Rafael Swell of eastern Utah. While mining for vanadium, ores that were too high in uranium content were often cast aside in waste dumps at the mine sites. A few years later, uranium from those waste dumps would jump start the American nuclear industry.

One of Moab's adopted sons, Howard Balsley, is considered by many to be the father of the uranium industry in the United States. Balsley came to Moab as a young man in 1908 and made his living as a forest ranger for many years. But he prospected, too, and helped others to develop uranium and vanadium mines in the early days of the twentieth century.

❋ ❋ ❋ ❋ ❋ ❋ ❋ ❋ ❋ ❋ ❋ ❋ ❋ ❋

balsley also kept more than a ton of highly radioactive carnotite ore behind his house in a shed for a few years during the 1950s. He told friends that the yellow mineral was just too pretty to sell. The radioactive rock in the shed would ping the Geiger counters of any prospector passing by, and several knocked on his door to tell him they had made a major discovery in his backyard. Balsley never seemed to suffer any ill effects from his long association with radioactive gases and dust. He died in 1982 at the age of 95. There is a funny story in town that, at his funeral, a woman was overheard to say, "That old uranium finally got him."

In the early 1930s, Balsley became a buyer and supplier of uranium and vanadium ores to the Vitro Manufacturing Company of Pittsburgh. In those days, Vitro used the ore primarily to make ceramic pigments to sell to glass and pottery manufacturers. Balsley contracted with dozens of small miners all over the Colorado Plateau to make up his fifty-ton contractual shipments. The ore supply was limited and the mines scattered. He bought colorful carnotite uranium ore by the ton and by the pound. Each shipment was loaded onto rail cars at Thompson Springs in one-hundred-pound sacks.

With the advent of World War II, the government began stockpiling strategic reserves of vanadium. Howard Balsley ran an ore-buying station in Moab. He bought radioactive material that was high in vanadium content from small producers all over southern Utah and western Colorado. The ore was shipped in open trucks to a processing mill in Durango, Colorado.

In the late 1940s, Balsley made trips to Washington, D.C., to meet with officials of the newly formed Atomic Energy Commission. Most of the nation's uranium was being imported from Canada and Africa at the time, and government bureaucrats didn't think there was enough uranium in the western United States to bother with. Balsley championed the Colorado Plateau as a place where America could find a good source of domestic uranium with just a little help from Uncle Sam. The miners needed roads, mills, and economic incentives. Balsley was instrumental in getting the government to do preliminary studies of the uranium potential of the Colorado Plateau. The rest is history. Moab's own Howard Balsley is the guy who lit the fuse for the Uranium Boom of the 1950s.

In the early 1950s, as the race for bomb-grade uranium shifted into high gear, Balsley's many years of experience in finding, mining, and marketing uranium secured him unofficial status as the Grand Master and Oracle of the uranium business. Hundreds of hopeful prospectors, government agents, and mine developers sought his advice and help. Balsley was a good guy, and shared his knowledge for free with anyone who asked.

The Yellow Circle Dream Mine

Everyone dreams of getting rich at one time or another, but some people really dream it—literally. One of the strangest stories to come out of Moab is the story of the Yellow Circle Dream Mine.

It began in 1915, when a man named Charles Snell went, with hat in hand, to speak to a Moab Forest Ranger named Howard Balsley about acquiring a grubstake—an arrangement where a benefactor pays the prospector's expenses for a share of any profits in the prospecting venture. Snell was broke, but he said he was sure he knew where a good uranium mine could be found. Strangely, this happened almost forty years before the Uranium Boom. But uranium had been mined in small quantities on the Colorado Plateau since 1879, and Madame Curie had purchased local ores for her experiments with radon. So uranium was known to have some market potential, even at that early date.

The thing that makes this story unique is that Charlie Snell had dreamed the location of the mine and freely admitted it when he asked Balsley for a grubstake. He said he saw the location in a dream and he recognized the canyon and the rock formation. He told Balsley that a yellow circle would be found in white sandstone at the location of the mineral vein, and he was sure he could find the place. All he needed was a little help with food and supplies.

As was the custom, the benefactor (Balsley) would share 50 percent of any profits from the prospecting venture for providing the grubstake. Balsley said he knew Snell to be an honest man, and so he gave him the things he needed. Even he couldn't have dreamed what would happen next.

Snell returned ten days later with a big smile and his pockets full of rocks. He reported that he had indeed found the yellow circle and a good vein of uranium ore, and had staked claims in his and Balsley's names. All they needed now was to mine the mineral and get rich. Unfortunately, there was not a big market for uranium in 1915. For the next several years, the mining claims produced nothing. Snell's dream of riches remained only a dream.

Years later came the Atomic Age, and uranium was king. The Yellow Circle Dream Mine became a million-dollar producer. Unfortunately, Howard Balsley sold his interest in the mine several years before it became profitable, and for a tiny fraction of what it was eventually worth.

Balsley did keep that chunk of white sandstone with the yellow circle as a memento. It resided in his flower garden for several years and then was donated to the Dan O'Laury Museum in Moab. The dream rock with the yellow circle can be seen in the museum today.

Charlie Snell might have had extrasensory perceptions beyond even his wildest dreams. It is interesting to note that he talked Balsley into grubstaking him to prospect in Lisbon Valley, too. He told Balsley that he was sure there was uranium there, and he thought he could find it. But in spite of his best efforts, he never did.

There was uranium in Lisbon Valley all right—the Mother Lode. But Snell didn't have a chance of finding it. It was almost eighty feet underground and wouldn't be found until Charlie Steen poked a hole in it with a drill steel in 1952.

The Atomic Age
Comes to Moab

The age of atomic bombs and atomic power was officially born in a flash of light and thunder that shook the little town of Alamogordo, New Mexico, in July 1945. That first mushroom cloud boiling upward into the atmosphere was a sign that the world would never be the same again. The atomic genie was out of the bottle. It was one small step of technical development for man, one giant leap of trouble for mankind. Nuclear power offered great potential for lighting cities and running industry, but sadly, most early efforts went to weapons development instead.

In the late 1940s, partly because of the efforts of people like Howard Balsley, the newly formed Atomic Energy Commission began a comprehensive search for domestic sources of uranium on the Colorado Plateau. Everyone knew there was uranium there, but no one knew how much. Government agents made surveys, produced maps, made estimates of potential reserves, and discussed ways to expedite development.

But since two atom bombs had been enough to bring the Japanese Empire to heel, and since America had a monopoly on nuclear technology, Uncle Sam didn't get too excited about large stockpiles of nuclear material until after the Russians detonated an A-bomb in

1949. After that, a nuclear arms race began in earnest. The United States didn't know how to counter the Soviet threat, so the army tried to intimidate the Russians by making bigger and "better" bombs—and lots more of them. Sadly, the Russians responded in kind.

With both sides stockpiling thousands of thermonuclear weapons, enough to destroy the world hundreds of times over, uranium was suddenly in high demand. There was power in the yellow mineral, and the he who possessed it controlled the fate of the world. Almost overnight, uranium became as valuable as diamonds and gold. To feed the nuclear bomb industry, there was an explosion of prospecting activity all across the American Southwest. It would be called the Uranium Boom, and Moab was Ground Zero.

the arms race became a reckless, mindless venture that threatened the very existence of life on the planet. We were fighting a "Cold War" with our fingers on the nuclear triggers. An end-of-the-world battle plan actually became official policy. The strategy was known as "Mutually Assured Destruction," appropriately shortened to the military acronym "MAD."

At first, the government only encouraged uranium prospecting and promised to buy the finished product. But with the growing shadow of the Soviet nuclear threat looming large on distant horizons, and with domestic uranium production remaining at only a trickle, it was decided to prime the pump. Beginning in 1951, the Atomic Energy Commission began a program of incentives to accelerate the race to Armageddon. The feds raised the price of uranium by nearly 300 percent and offered a $10,000 bounty for each significant new discovery. Ten grand doesn't sound like a lot of money today, but in 1951, ten thousand bucks would buy a nice house. The agency also agreed to help pay the costs of transporting ore from the mine to the mill, and promised to buy the ore for a minimum of ten years. It was a sweet deal—a carrot on a stick.

To help even more, Uncle Sam bulldozed dozens of roads into wilderness areas to "open" the backcountry for uranium exploration. At the same time, government offices began to distribute brochures and maps with helpful hints on how and where to find radioactive minerals. Uranium processing mills were established near Monticello, about fifty-five miles south of Moab, and at White Canyon, near Hite.

It was the first time the federal government actively participated in a "gold rush," and all of the propaganda suggested that is was relatively easy to get rich. All a fellow had to do was quit his day job, invest his life savings in a jeep and a camp outfit, and find a pocket of yellow ore out there among the red rocks—nothing to it. Thousands took the bait.

The desert was soon full of hopeful, novice prospectors, and more than a few professionals. People were scrambling all over the canyons, ledges, mesas, and creek bottoms with Geiger counters and high hopes. And then, in the summer of 1952, came word of Charlie Steen's fabulously rich find at Mi Vida, just a few miles south of Moab (more on this coming up). The race for uranium shifted into overdrive.

With Charlie Steen's smiling face in dozens of magazines and newspapers, uranium prospecting around Moab hit a fever pitch that equaled the California gold rush. A steady stream of hopeful prospectors became a raging flood. People came from every state and several foreign countries. Schoolteachers, bankers, bus drivers, barbers, cooks, clerks, cops, and cowboys quit their jobs, cashed in their government savings bonds, and took to the hills. Everyone wanted to be rich like Charlie Steen.

There was pandemonium on the desert. People staked claims everywhere. Wild-eyed would-be millionaires dashed hither and thither with Geiger counters, shovels, and rock hammers, chasing daydreams and radioactive rumors. Some people were greedy, and there were fistfights, gunfights, dogfights, and court fights. Hundreds of small uranium companies were organized, some with no assets at all. Salt Lake City became the nation's center for speculating in uranium industry penny stocks.

Moab was not ready for the Uranium Boom. She was caught completely by surprise. During the 1940s, Moab had been a sleepy little cow town populated primarily by the children of her pioneer ancestors. Everyone knew everyone else and there were few "strangers" in town. Agriculture and ranching were primary industries. Life was quiet, laid-back, and slow. The town was rural America at its best, a place Norman Rockwell would have loved to paint.

But ready or not, Moab found itself in the bulls-eye of the nuclear arms race. The town exploded. The population went from one thousand to almost six thousand between 1953 and 1956. Services, infrastructure, and logistics were stretched beyond the limits. A trailer town spilled from Main Street down toward the river, and dozens—maybe hundreds—more people camped out near the edges of town.

Newspapers and magazines were soon calling Moab "The Uranium Capital of the World," and the town was quick to capitalize on the notoriety. Soon there were "Uranium Capital of the World" signs all over town. Almost every business and storefront had the words "Uranium" or "Atomic" stenciled on signs or the sides of the buildings.

By the late1950s, city fathers were able to bring some order to the boomtown development. Charlie Steen bought much of the land west and north of town and created a housing development the locals called Steenville. Many of the Steenville residents worked for Steen's various business enterprises.

road building on federal lands was unregulated, and anyone could drop the blade of a bulldozer and cut a trail across the wilderness to a promising mine site. No environmental impact assessments were ever done and no archaeological surveys undertaken. Only God knows what was destroyed or plowed under. Little shantytown mining camps sprang up in the canyons everywhere, and trash was thrown over canyon rims or tossed into shallow streambeds. Many of the scars and trash piles are still with us today.

Slowly Moab was able to absorb the influx of new people. The Boom was good for business, and Moab would never again be the sleepy little town she had once been. Times changed, the world changed, and Moab changed. There were new people, new businesses, and a new mindset in

Moab's Uranium Queen, 1956
(Museum of Moab photo BS-1)

town. Moab had been propelled into the twentieth century. Today, many of Moab's permanent residents are children of the Uranium Boom whose parents came to find atomic treasure and stayed because they liked the town and loved the country.

The story of the Uranium Boom is well documented. It was probably the last time our nation will ever see anything like a gold rush on public lands. Some see it as a shameful time of unregulated rape and exploitation of the environment and our natural resources. To others, it was the last gasp of the old West. Either way, there was no better place to host the event than the little frontier town of Moab, Utah.

Charlie Steen,
the Uranium King

No story about Moab is complete without discussing the town's most famous character. Charlie Steen was bigger than life in the 1950s, and he's the guy who put Moab on the map. His story is fascinating—rags to riches and back to rags again, the American dream with a twist of lemon.

Charles Augustus Steen was born in Texas in 1919. He was a geologist by trade, educated at the Texas School of Mines. After graduating from college, he worked the Texas oil patch for a while, but he couldn't stay with a job for very long. He was a free spirit who had trouble with bosses. He was headstrong and didn't take orders well.

In December 1949, Charlie was out of work. While hanging around the house, he read an article in one of his geology periodicals about the government's new interest in domestic sources of uranium. With the dawning of the Cold War and the Atomic Age, uranium had become a strategic mineral, vital to national defense. The article said that uranium could be found on the Colorado Plateau, and the government would buy all that could be processed. Unemployed Charlie was charmed. He was, after all, a professional geologist. If anyone could find the radioactive pot of gold at the end of the rainbow, it would be Charlie Steen.

Steen secured a $1,000 grubstake from his mother, loaded up his wife and three little boys (a fourth son would be born the next year), and moved to Utah. For a couple of years, the family lived in a rented tarpaper shack in the tiny semi-ghost town of Cisco, about fifty miles northeast of Moab. Things were tough, and the family lived a hand-to-mouth existence. Steen often poached deer to help feed his family. Every possible dollar went for drill steels, gasoline, and other prospecting supplies.

For two long years, Charlie was able to keep going through merchants who extended credit and by securing grubstakes from adventurous friends and acquaintances. Charlie Steen and his beat-up old red jeep were in Moab often, looking for another grubstake. Some folks, including government agents, began referring to the down-and-out prospector from Texas as the "Cisco Kid."

But the Cisco Kid got the last laugh. He was the guy who found the Mother Lode. The story is a good one, for the Atomic Energy Commission had written the area off. Official government geologists insisted there could be no high-grade uranium there. They smiled and spoke of "Steen's folly" when

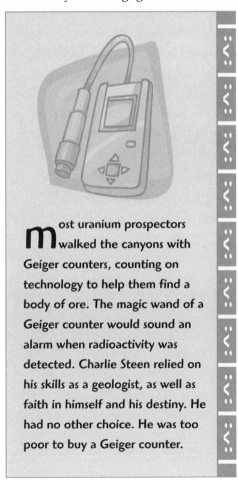

most uranium prospectors walked the canyons with Geiger counters, counting on technology to help them find a body of ore. The magic wand of a Geiger counter would sound an alarm when radioactivity was detected. Charlie Steen relied on his skills as a geologist, as well as faith in himself and his destiny. He had no other choice. He was too poor to buy a Geiger counter.

Charlie, a professional geologist, too, insisted that there should be a bed of radioactive ore somewhere in the Big Indian Mining District.

On July 27, 1952, Charlie's borrowed drill rig broke down after boring through a thick layer of black rock, seventy-three feet beneath the sandstone of Lisbon Valley, about thirty-five miles south of Moab. Discouraged and thoroughly down in the dumps, he threw his tools, along with fragments of the black rock, into his jeep and made his way back to Cisco.

At Cisco he stopped for gas before going home. He wasn't anxious to tell his wife, Minnie Lee (who preferred to be called by her initials, M.L.), that another week of drilling had been a failure. While at the service station, he told station owner and fellow prospecting enthusiast Buddy Cowger about his bad luck. Cowger just happened to have a Geiger counter nearby, and on a whim, he put a chunk of the black rock under the wand and turned it on.

The machine shrieked and the needle pegged off the clock. Charlie was stunned. He had unknowingly found pitchblende—radioactive uraninite. The ore was high grade and worth a king's ransom. Charlie had drilled through fourteen feet of the stuff. Uraninite had never been found in commercial quantities in the United States before and the young geologist hadn't recognized the mineral. He was expecting to find yellow carnotite.

Charlie left his jeep sitting at the gas pumps and, waving a chunk of pitchblende in his hand, took a shortcut, jumping fences and nearly tearing his head off when he hit a clothesline on his way to tell M.L. and the kids that they were rich. Their lives would never be the same again. The years of poverty and faith had paid off—big time.

Charlie's claim in Lisbon Valley was appropriately named Mi Vida (Spanish for "My Life"). In the first six months of production, Steen shipped a million dollars worth of ore. He was suddenly rich and famous, and he became the poster boy of the Uranium Boom. His picture was everywhere. The Mi Vida and the surrounding Big Indian Mining District would ship more than ten million tons of ore, worth more than a billion dollars, over the next 30 years.

With his newfound wealth, Steen moved his family to Moab and had a marvelous house constructed on the hillside northeast of town. The house, which cost the ungodly sum of $250,000, was a little ostentatious for rural Utah in 1953. Steen also bought a red Lincoln

Charlie Steen with three of his four sons shortly after finding the largest bed of high-grade uranium ore ever discovered in Utah. The battered old jeep was his prospecting vehicle. (Photo courtesy of the Western Railroad and Mining Museum in Helper, Utah)

automobile and a few airplanes. He enjoyed his money and his reputation as a rebel who prevailed against the odds. The Cisco Kid was
now the King of Uranium, and the world beat a path to his door.

Legend has it that Steen refused to let some government geologists tour his mines, saying something like: "You guys know there's no
ore in the Big Indian District." The Cisco Kid harbored a touch of
malice toward those who had ridiculed and made fun of him. But the
man was compassionate too. He was generous to people who had
befriended him, extended credit, and grubstaked him in his hour of
need. He made sure that Buddy Cowger and others who had helped
him were given an opportunity to stake claims alongside his own
before word of the fabulous find became public knowledge. Some of
those mining claims made millions for their owners. Steen also
donated many acres of land and many thousands of dollars to community projects and worthy causes. He gave $50,000 for a new
hospital in Moab, and paid to expand the town's waterworks. He
threw an annual party for the whole town that cost him tens of thousands of dollars. His parties, held in an aircraft hangar, were attended
by as many as eight thousand people and were the talk of southern
Utah for years to come.

* * *

"Leave it to Beaver"
at Ten Thousand Feet

*There are many stories about the eccentricities of Charlie Steen, the
Uranium King. After the man made his millions, he sometimes indulged
himself in ways not available to the common folk. Steen loved airplanes,
and it is said that once a week he flew his family to Salt Lake City for
rumba lessons and shopping.*

*But one of the most incredible tales has to do with television. In the
1950s, television signals were captured with antennas on top of individual*

 houses, and Moab, being down in a canyon and surrounded by mountains, did not get good TV reception. So, it is said, when the time rolled around to view a favorite TV program, the Steen family would journey to the airport with pillows and snacks and take to the sky. There they would orbit the most beautiful country in the world while watching black-and-white TV in the dark cabin of the airplane.

For an hour or two, they would soar over red-rock deserts, craggy mountain peaks covered with snow, dark green forest glades, and deeply shadowed river canyons. The plane would float through the clear evening sky, amid billowing clouds and fiery sunsets, where the TV signal was much, much better.

The Ecstasy and the Agony

For a few years, everything Steen touched turned to gold—or better yet, yellow uranium. He founded the UTEX Corporation and the Uranium Reduction Company that constructed the uranium-processing mill along the river north of Moab. He also owned the Moab Drilling Company, Big Indian Mines, Inc., the Mi Vida Company, Standard Uranium Corporation, and several other businesses. Through his many ventures, Steen became Grand County's largest employer for a few years. He also owned a good chunk of Moab real estate. In 1958 his name and reputation got him elected to the Utah State Senate.

But the King of Uranium did not get along well in the Mormon-controlled state legislature. Steen was a sociable fellow who saw nothing wrong with a little nightcap once in a while. The Mormons are teetotalers, observing the "Word of Wisdom," which is a religious dietary law similar to the one introduced by Moses in the Old Testament. Alcohol, coffee, tea, and tobacco are taboo to Mormons.

Unfortunately, the principal target of Charlie Steen's ambitions at the state legislature was to change what he perceived to be Utah's unreasonable liquor laws. Bravely, he proposed legislation to allow liquor by the drink (over the counter). It was blasphemy to the LDS faithful who controlled the state legislature, and he got almost no support. Stung by what he perceived to be a personal affront, Charlie resigned from the Utah Senate in 1961.

After his misadventure in Utah politics, Steen decided to move to Nevada. In Nevada he could buy liquor by the drink, and the State of Nevada had no state income tax. Charlie sold his mine and other Utah business interests in 1962 and rode off into the sunset. He had a bigger and more ambitious mansion constructed on a large estate near Reno. The new house covered twenty-seven thousand square feet.

Unfortunately, Charlie's luck stayed in Utah when he moved to Nevada. The former uranium king invested heavily in risky projects and ended up losing his shirt. The man was a gambler, a taker of risks, and he got into projects that took his money without giving anything back. He bought horses that didn't win, real estate that didn't sell, a pickle factory that went sour, a marble quarry that went under, a cattle ranch that didn't pay, and he got into the propeller-driven airplane manufacturing business when everyone was deciding they wanted jets. He put his best efforts into diversifying his portfolio, but mining and milling were what he knew best, and he had sold his uranium money tree. By 1968 he was broke. It took eleven years to settle with the U.S. government over back taxes.

After declaring bankruptcy, Charlie went back to prospecting. If he could do it once, he could do it twice. But sadly, it was not to be. In 1971, while drilling for copper ore in California, he was badly injured when hit in the head by a broken drill steel. He was in a coma for a month, almost died, and never fully recovered.

In 1992, the town of Moab held a parade and a party for Charlie Steen and his wife, M.L., to celebrate the fortieth anniversary of his big strike. People also wanted to thank him for his many contributions to the town and the area. It was a bittersweet celebration. Only a few dusty bones of his fortune remained, and his family was torn apart fighting over the scraps.

After suffering with Alzheimer's disease for many years, Charlie Steen died on New Year's Day, 2006, at the age of 86. He died a heroic but tragic figure worthy of a Shakespearian play. Few men

a vestige of Steen's glory days can still be found and visited in Moab. It is called the Sunset Grill. The restaurant is in Steen's old house on the hill where, for a few short years, the King of Uranium looked down on his empire.

have ever experienced such good luck and such bad luck, such triumph and such tragedy. But through it all, he lived life to the fullest, brave enough to chase his dreams. And when buffeted by the ill winds of fate, he suffered the slings and arrows of cruel misfortune with as much dignity as he could muster. He was one of Moab's most colorful characters, and his memory will live forever.

Give Me a Home Where the Millionaires Roam

By 1956 Moab was firmly established as the "Uranium Capital of the World." A sign boldly announced that fact at the entrance to town, and the masthead of the local newspaper sported a drawing of an atomic configuration with the same slogan. Uranium was king, and Moab was king of uranium.

With radioactive notoriety came great wealth. Those who owned the mines and mills made a killing. Charlie Steen is the best-known example, but there were others who made fortunes in the business without ever stepping into the spotlight. Several of Steen's business partners were among them.

In the December 1956 issue of *McCall's Magazine*, Elizabeth Pope wrote an article about Moab entitled "The Richest Town in the U.S.A." In the article, Pope proclaimed that Moab had the largest concentration of millionaires in the country. The town had a population slightly less than six thousand, but twenty to thirty millionaires resided within the city limits.

If the numbers were true, Moab had a millionaire population density fifty times the national average for the 1950s. Not bad for a dusty little town in the desert. And not surprisingly, there is still some disagreement about what the millionaire count really was. It is said that some of the people counted as millionaires had assets "on paper" only, and the wealth disappeared when the Uranium Boom went bust.

It was hard to spot a Moab millionaire at the time. Most of the atomic millionaires lived quiet, unpretentious lives. They lived in modest homes, drove reasonably modest cars, and dressed and acted like the rest of the natives. Charlie Steen is the one glaring exception. His mansion on the hill, his widely publicized philanthropy, his stint as state senator, and his annual town parties set him apart from the others.

The one weakness that all of the Moab millionaires seemed to share was a love of airplanes. Moab was still semi-isolated in the days when the glow of the radioactive rainbow touched the center of town. Even the best paved roads in eastern Utah were long, winding, and bad, and for a few years, Moab's little airport in Spanish Valley was one of Utah's busiest.

An Atomic Legacy

The Uranium Boom of the 1950s changed the town and the Land of Moab forever. The town gained a certain measure of notoriety, and the land was no longer an empty spot on the map. Moab's population had grown 500 percent in less than five years, and for the first time, newcomers with roots in different towns, states, and countries outnumbered the children of Moab's pioneers. There were dozens of new businesses and a much more diversified economy. Farming, ranching, and small-time mining were no longer the only games in town.

There were also many scars upon the land. Old prospecting roads wandered aimlessly across the wilderness. Mineshafts dotted canyon walls with gaping holes that looked down on desert valleys like the empty eye sockets of skulls, crying tears of mine rubble. Trash, rusting old automobiles, and worn-out mine machinery lay strewn about the old mine sites. The skeletons of tarpaper shacks and weather-beaten old camp trailers slowly decayed in the hot desert sun. The wind moaned through gaps and fissures in the old buildings, toying with ragged strips of tarpaper and whistling down empty chimney pipes. Everywhere there were knee-high piles of rocks that had been claim markers, sad and abandoned monuments holding down the corners of someone's failed field of dreams. And closer to town, an atomic nightmare was slowly creeping into people's consciousness.

In 1956 Charlie Steen had formed the Uranium Reduction Company (URECO). The purpose of the company was to construct and operate a uranium-processing mill on land Steen owned along the Colorado River about three miles north of Moab. It was an ambitious project, the first independently owned uranium mill in the country. The facility was designed primarily to process the high-grade pitchblende ores from Steen's mines in Lisbon Valley, but it did accommodate the milling of other mine ores, too.

In those days there were few environmental regulations, and waste from the mill was slurried into unlined evaporation ponds along the floodplain of the river. The slurry was laced with high levels of radioactive waste, ammonia, and various acids and chemicals used in the uranium extraction process. It was a toxic atomic soup that slowly condensed in the shallow, dirt-banked ponds and seeped into the ground near the river.

The Atlas Corporation bought the facility when Steen moved to Nevada in 1962, and the company continued to operate the plant

<> <> <> <> <> <> <> <> <>

the sheer volume of radioactive waste has made the site one of the nation's top candidates for superfund environmental cleanup. The close proximity of the town, the nearby visitor's center of Arches National Park, groundwater contamination, airborne dust concerns, and pollution of the Colorado River have been major concerns. And yet, incredibly, the monstrous pile of toxic waste has continued to loom over the landscape since the mill was closed in 1984. The site is only half a mile from the entrance to Arches National Park, and it is the first trace of Moab one sees when approaching the town from the north.

until 1984. By the time the mill was closed, the tailings pile had grown to cover 130 acres to a height of 110 feet. Counting contaminated dirt where the mill itself once stood, it is estimated that there might be as many as sixteen million tons of toxic waste at the site.

After closing the mill, Atlas Minerals proposed to the Nuclear Regulatory Commission (NRC) that the company be allowed to cover the tailings pile with dirt and walk away. But after much study and debate, the government determined that the greatest environmental danger is contamination of groundwater and the river, problems that a cap of dirt will not fix. The pile is also on the floodplain of the river, subjected to floods, unstable soil conditions, and migrating riverbanks.

Studies and alternative plans were debated and negotiated between Atlas Minerals and the NRC for years. And in 1995, Atlas did cover the tailings pile with dirt as a temporary measure. But finally, faced with an estimated hundred million dollars in costs to stabilize the material in place or move it to a safer location, Atlas Minerals filed for bankruptcy in 1998. With that action, responsibility for taking care of the problem fell to the NRC.

The NRC had not the budget nor the resources to handle the problem, and an act of Congress transferred responsibility to the Department of Energy (DOE) in October 2000. The legislation required the DOE to consult with the National Academy of Sciences to determine the best solution to the hazardous waste problem.

After a final Environmental Impact Statement was released in 2005, the DOE issued a Record of Decision in September of that year. It was decided to move the tailings pile and other contaminated soil thirty-five miles north to Crescent Junction. There, approximately twenty-three hundred acres of public lands have been set aside to construct a disposal cell, roads, and support facilities. Eventually, the DOE plans to release all but about 260 acres of the land back to the public domain. The permanent waste site will be just north of Interstate 70. It is expected that construction of the containment cell will begin in 2007, and the DOE hopes to have the Moab site cleaned up by 2014. The material will be shipped using the existing railroad spur that links the D&RGW line near Crescent Junction with the potash mine near Moab.

Uranium brought Moab its greatest period of economic prosperity and its most serious encounter with environmental degradation. The "Uranium Capital of the World" experienced the best and the worst that the uranium business and the Atomic Age could offer. And in recent years, there has been talk about a possible resurgence of uranium mining and milling in the area—this time, hopefully, for the generation of nuclear power and not for the making of bombs.

As could be expected, the possibility of a new Uranium Boom has met with mixed reviews. A few big corporations are optimistic. A few environmental groups are preparing to do battle. Government agents and agencies, so far, have not committed publicly either way. Politicians are being cautious, waiting to see which way the winds of public sentiment will blow. And most citizens of eastern Utah are willing to do it all again. After all, there are jobs and economic prosperity at the end of the radioactive rainbow.

Where the nuclear business might go in the next few years is anybody's guess. But one thing we can be sure of—the days of slap-dash, mindlessly tearing the world apart to find buried treasure are gone. The days of dumping hazardous waste in piles for someone else to clean up are gone, too. People will demand better accountability this time.

And while the uranium mining and milling business lies sleeping like a dormant volcano for the time being, the mining industry is not completely dead in the Land of Moab. There is another, non-nuclear mining venture in the area that has outlasted the uranium business and prospered for more than forty years. It is the Cane Creek Potash Mine, located about twenty miles west of Moab along the Colorado River. The mine employs about fifty people and produces approximately 100,000 tons of potash and about 150,000 tons of other mineral salts per year.

Mineral potash is an impure form of potassium carbonate and is used primarily as a fertilizer today. Several potassium compounds can be derived from mineral potash, and historically, potash was used in the manufacture of glass, soap, and even gunpowder. For centuries a form of potash was made from water-soluble wood ash.

The Cane Creek (Intrepid) Potash Mine was first opened in 1964 as a conventional underground mine with a room-and-pillar mining plan. But in 1970 it was converted to a solution-mining and solar-evaporation operation. Water is pumped from the nearby Colorado River through injection wells to about the three-thousand-foot level of the mine, where the water dissolves the potash and mineral salts. The potash brine is then pumped back to the surface and sent to a four-hundred-acre evaporation site southwest of the mine. The evaporation ponds can be seen from the view area at Dead Horse Point State Park. The mine is situated in the beautiful Colorado River canyon, and the Moab Potash Road is often listed as one of the scenic attractions of the area.

A blue dye similar to food coloring is added to the brine water in the evaporation ponds to facilitate a faster evaporation rate. The dye gives the pond water a deep, ocean blue color. The ponds are lined with heavy vinyl to prevent any of the slurry from seeping into the ground water or the nearby river. Once a cell has completed the evaporation process, the minerals are scooped up using heavy equipment and sent through a processing plant where the potash and salts are separated, refined, and bagged. The final products are shipped by rail. Unlike the uranium business, no hazardous materials are used or produced anywhere in the process.

National Parks and National Treasures

o other place in America has more square miles tied up in national parks, national monuments, national recreation areas, national forests, state parks, and Indian reservations than the area around Moab. Millions of tourists come to the area every year to sightsee, hike, bike, explore, and enjoy the natural wonders.

The whole area is blessed with a rugged beauty that anyone with a soul can delight in. The massive rock formations, the broken and twisted canyons, the majesty of snowcapped mountains, the placid, big river with shimmering reflections of ledges, clouds, and sky are unsurpassed anywhere. The very colors of the sky, the rocks, and the dirt itself are magnificent. But even in this land of unsurpassed beauty, some areas are more spectacular than others.

As early as 1917, the Moab newspaper was printing stories about a special place of scenic wonders in the sandstone rims and canyons north of town. There were rumors of huge sandstone arches, bridges, and spires. But in those early years, travel was difficult, and few people made the effort to visit. For more than fifty years, from 1880 into the early 1930s, the scenic wonderland that would become Arches National Park was the private domain, workspace, and playground of a few lucky cowboys.

The Turnbow (Wolfe Ranch) cabin at Arches National Park, 1918
(Museum of Moab photo 44-30)

In the 1890s, a man named John Wolfe homesteaded on Salt Wash, near the present trailhead to Delicate Arch. An old log cabin, the Wolfe Ranch house, is still standing and can be visited at the site. Wolfe sold his holdings to Marvin Turnbow in the early 1900s, and while Turnbow and his family were busy tending cows and living in the log cabin, their front yard was "discovered" and brought to the national limelight.

It all began in 1923, when a man named Alexander Ringhoffer contacted railroad officials with a proposal to promote the Salt Valley and Salt Wash areas as a tourist destination. While prospecting, Ringhoffer had found a place he called the "Devil's Garden," and he was sure that other people would want to see it, too. Railroad bosses were always looking for ways to sell more tickets, and they were interested in the possibilities. Ringhoffer took a group of railroad people on a tour of the area, and the scenery knocked their socks off. With some enthusiasm, the railroad tycoons lent their considerable political clout to the project, and in 1929, Herbert Hoover designated 4,520 acres of Marvin Turnbow's scenic front yard as Arches National Monument. It was a humble beginning.

But even after Arches was designated a national monument, the hoped-for tourist boom was slow in coming. Access was by horseback or by following the often-washed-out or sand-bogged Willow Springs wagon road. There were no facilities, no visitors' center, and few signs. Tourists camped in tents and cooked over open fires. Visitors were on their own, come what may. The first automobiles didn't claw their way into the monument until the mid-1930s.

In 1938 legislation was signed expanding the monument to almost thirty-four thousand acres (55 square miles), and the dirt road was improved. By 1947 a whopping forty-seven hundred visitors stopped by in a single year. In 1958 a new and less treacherous access road was shot through the sandstone ledges on the south end of the monument, and by 1959 Arches had enough visitors to justify a visitors' center. In 1964, the year nearby Canyonlands National Park was created, visitation topped one hundred thousand for the first time.

In 1971 Arches National Monument became Arches National Park, and the boundaries were expanded to more than seventy-six thousand acres

The original monument did not include the Turnbow (Wolfe) Ranch, and Marvin Turnbow was hired to work as a "caretaker" for the monument. It is interesting to note, too, that Alexander Ringhoffer's "Devil's Garden" was misplaced by a screw-up when the monument was first surveyed. Ringhoffer's Devil's Garden is known today as the Klondike Bluffs. The place marked as Devil's Garden on modern maps is about five miles to the east. But it really doesn't matter. The devil didn't have a garden in Arches anyway. Only angels of the desert live in such a marvelous place.

A view from Arches National Park with the La Sal Mountains in background
(author photo)

(123 square miles). Since then it has become a jewel in the crown of the national park system. Visitation exceeded 782,000 in 2005.

There are other parks and monuments in the area, too. In 1959 the State of Utah created a state park at Dead Horse Point, a spectacular overlook some two thousand feet above the Colorado River that looks down on the northern end of Canyonlands National Park. It is a photographer's delight and a great place to spend an afternoon. The scenery and the colors change constantly with the shadows and light conditions.

In the 1930s, and again in the 1950s, a national park was proposed for the Colorado River canyons below Moab. The region had long been known as a scenic wonderland, but it was terribly remote. The area didn't have the roads and other amenities to support a national park, and besides, in the 1950s, the Uranium Boom was in full swing and much of the proposed area was covered with mineral claims and dog-hole uranium mines. Economics and national security trumped wilderness and parks in the early days of the Cold War.

But the long-sought Colorado River park finally became a reality in the 1960s. It happened in conjunction with the creation of the Glen Canyon Dam and Lake Powell. The dam was authorized by Congress in 1956. The first concrete was poured in 1960, and the floodgates were closed in 1963, creating a reservoir 186 miles long with more shoreline than the entire west coast of the United States. The reservoir was named Lake Powell, after John Wesley Powell, who explored the area and wrote prolifically about its beauty (more on him later), but it's a sad thing, really. Old John Wesley Powell might have been angry had he known that Congress would attach his name to a reservoir that drowned his beloved Glen Canyon.

Canyonlands National Park was created in 1964, as the cold waters of Lake Powell were creeping over the river glades and Indian ruins of Glen Canyon. Eight years later, the Glen Canyon National Recreation Area became a reality. To improve access to the area, two modern paved highways, U95 and U276, were hammered through the sandstone of southern Utah as part of the state's bicentennial project. The roads were completed in the late 1970s. Today, Lake Powell and Canyonlands absorb an estimated two million visitors annually.

And so Moab sits amid a triangle of national treasures: Arches to the north, Dead Horse Point to the west, and Canyonlands and Lake Powell to the south. To the east towers the La Sal mountain range—the Elk Mountains of history and legend—a treasure in its own right.

The parks and Lake Powell are impressive, but in reality, all of southeastern Utah, from Interstate 70 south to Monument Valley and from the Colorado border westward to the San Rafael Swell, could easily qualify for national park status. The whole area is a scenic wonderland. There is no other place on earth quite like it.

▲ ▲ ▲

An Arch, a Bridge, or a Hole in the Wall?

The following is a list of commonly used terms for identifying rock features in the Moab and Canyonlands area:

A Window is a hole in a wall of rock.

A Bridge is a hole though rock with water running through it.

An Arch is like a bridge, but with no water running through it.

Slickrock is smooth, bare sandstone.

A Plateau is a mountain with a flat top.

*A Mesa is a high, steep-sided, small plateau. Mesa means "table"
in Spanish. Think of mesas in that way.*

A Butte is a small mesa.

A Bluff is a steep hill or cliff with a broad, rounded front.

A Ridge is a long, elevated piece of land.

A Pinnacle is a slender, freestanding shaft of rock.

*A Promontory is understood to be any high point of rock that protrudes
out over a canyon or other low-lying area.*

An Escarpment is a steep slope or cliff below a ridge, mesa, or plateau.

*The Book Cliffs is a name given to a particular large escarpment in
eastern Utah. The geologic layers of rock are clearly exposed and
resemble the pages of a closed book, or a stack of books, as seen
from the edge.*

The Name is Wilson Arch
—Damn It

Wilson Arch is about twenty-two miles south of Moab along Highway 191. It is an impressive arch and easily accessible. It is also fairly large. According to a local newspaper, a helicopter was flown through the arch in 1968.

The scenic wonder was called "Wilson Arch" for many years, but in the early 1960s, federal highway officials decided that "Window Arch" would be a better name. They officially registered their "better" name in Washington, D.C., and highway signs were painted proclaiming the site to be Window Arch.

People from Moab and Monticello were outraged. Their champion, Utah state senator Sam Taylor, went to the mat with the highway department and the federal government—and won. After much politicking, the name was officially changed back to Wilson Arch. It would seem to be much ado about nothing, but it was important to the local people to preserve the proper name. For you see, Wilson Arch was named for a special person in southeastern Utah.

It all began in 1880, when the Wilson brothers, Ervin and fourteen-year-old Joe, were sent by their father to drive a herd of cows from Moab to the La Sal Mountains. The boys were attacked by Indians at the south end of Spanish Valley. Details are not known, but the older brother, Ervin, escaped the ambush and rode to the

Wilson Arch (author photo)

town of La Sal some twenty miles to the south. Little Joe Wilson was not so lucky.

Joe was shot through the foot while running away. The heavy, muzzle-loading bullet took off "half his foot." Unable to run any farther, and losing a lot of blood, he tried to play dead. Suspecting that the boy was playing possum, an Indian shot him square in the face from point-blank range. The bullet passed through his nose, taking out his cheekbone and one eye. Satisfied that he was dead, the Indians rode away, leaving him for the buzzards.

But Joe was not dead. Terribly wounded, the boy managed to crawl "partway" back to Moab before he was found by a group of "friendly" Indians. The friendly Indians, afraid that they might be blamed for the boy's injuries, took him to a settler's cabin after dark and left him in the yard. They made noise to alert the pioneer family and then vanished in the night.

Incredibly, the boy recovered in those days before hospitals, antibiotics, or plastic surgeons, but he limped badly for the rest of his life and his face was horribly disfigured. He never married or had a family. In later years, he homesteaded a piece of desert in Dry Valley near the arch and desert canyon that still bear his name, and he lived there in seclusion to the end of his days.

Joe Wilson died the way he lived—all alone. A passing cowboy found him dead in his cabin. Wilson Arch is his memorial. It is no wonder that people from Moab wouldn't let the highway department change the name.

The Real Faux Falls

About ten miles south of Moab is a wonderful waterfall. The sparkling water tumbles and spills down a steep, red-rock hillside for a few hundred feet. The contrasting colors are beautiful, and the roar, splash, and tinkle of falling water a delight in the harsh desert environment. People enjoy the place, and in recent years, the falls have become one of the most photographed sites in Grand County outside of the national parks.

But while the falls are very real, some accuse them of being contrived. For you see, Faux Falls, as they have come to be known, are man made. The water is diverted from Mill Creek and sent through the sandstone spine of Brumley Ridge in a tunnel. On the west side of the ridge, the water pours out into the warm sunshine and then bounces happily down the hillside on its way to find Ken's Lake, a reservoir, in the valley below. It is part of a county water project that provides recreational opportunities for the community and irrigation water for about five hundred acres of Spanish Valley farmland.

The project was conceived in pioneer times, but not completed until 1981. The reservoir provides some fishing and boating activities, and there are well-maintained campsites in a fee area near the reservoir. A footpath leads up the hillside for those who want a closer look at the unique and lovely Faux Falls.

Faux Falls, about ten miles south of Moab
(author photo)

A "Point" of Politeness

Dead Horse Point is a narrow promontory some two thousand feet above the Colorado River, a few miles west of Moab. The place offers spectacular views of the river and the canyon country. In 1959 the State of Utah made Dead Horse Point a state park.

The park is a place of stories, legends, and lies, and is best known in recent years as the place substituted for the Grand Canyon in the 1991 movie *Thelma and Louise*. In that classic, feminists-gone-wild film, the girls and their red T-Bird go over the canyon just north of the park boundary. Any scenic overlook that can serve as proxy for the Grand Canyon is worth the time to visit.

As to the name of the place, the lingering tale is that somehow a herd of wild horses was stranded out on that narrow neck of land and either died of thirst or jumped from the ledges trying to get to the river for a drink. Some stories say the horses got there by themselves, and others say they were corralled there by outlaws or misguided cowboys who never went back to take them to water.

Sam Taylor, longtime editor of the *Times-Independent* newspaper, offers another possibility. According to Taylor, an old cowboy story says that somewhere northeast of the present overlook site, there used to be some large potholes in the sandstone, many feet deep. The holes would fill with water during the winter months or after a good rain. Wildlife and livestock would drink from those deep natural "tanks." But as summers wore long and the potholes began to dry up, horses would reach deeper and deeper for a drink, and would sometimes slip and fall into the waterholes, where they died. Tired of losing good cowponies in that manner, ranchers filled the potholes with rocks, trees, and brush to keep the horses out.

Taylor also quotes an old cowboy who once told him, "They weren't horses at all. They were burros. But they couldn't name the place Dead A___ Point." Taylor is a gentleman, and "A___" is the way he wrote it.

Moab Goes to the Movies

I n the 1930s, Hollywood discovered Monument Valley. It was the era of Westerns, and some of the most colorful scenery in the world was used as a backdrop for early black-and-white cowboy films. It didn't matter. Even in shades of gray, the Utah desert is spectacular.

But by 1949, after doing four classic westerns in Monument Valley, director John Ford was searching for a new location with similar landscapes. A few miles to the north, he discovered the Land of Moab. After consulting with Bish Taylor, editor of the Moab newspaper, Ford was introduced to George White, a local rancher and Grand County promoter. White took the Hollywood scout on a tour of the Moab area, pointing out the scenery, the varied panoramas, the natural technicolor, textures, shadows, and moods of the desert. The movie man melted. Ford agreed to do his next movie, *Wagonmaster*, in the scenic splendor around Moab. The rest is history.

Logistics were a nightmare in those early days. Moab had about twelve hundred residents, and the influx of the movie crews required the erection of a tent city. There was just no space for that many visitors. Some of the movie stars and high-status production people were housed in private homes. A catering service from California was hired to help feed the movie crews.

Recognizing the economic potential of the movie industry for the small community, George White recruited local business and civic leaders to be part of a "movie committee" to help with coordination, logistics, public relations, and problem solving. The informal, all-volunteer organization eventually became the "Moab Film Commission." The commission was instrumental in promoting the town and attracting many more movie companies to the area.

Hollywood fell in love with the scenery around Moab. The area had everything a big-screen moviemaker could ask for: magnificent landscapes, towering snow-capped mountains, canyons and ledges of red-rock splendor, and a river that ran through it. Since John Ford's hopeful beginning in 1949, dozens of movies have been filmed in the area. Some of the more notable are:

- 1949—*Wagonmaster*, with Ben Johnson, Harry Carey Jr., and Joanne Dru

- 1950—*Rio Grande*, with John Wayne and Maureen O'Hara

- 1952—*Battle at Apache Pass*, with Jeff Chandler

- 1953—*The Siege at Red River*, with Van Johnson and Joanne Dru

- 1953—*Taza, Son of Cochise*, with Rock Hudson, Jeff Chandler, and Barbara Rush

- 1954—*Smoke Signal*, with Piper Laurie and Dana Andrews

- 1956—*Fort Dobbs*, with Clint Walker and Virginia Mayo

- 1958—*Warlock*, with Henry Fonda, Anthony Quinn, and Dorothy Malone

- 1959—*Ten Who Dared*, with Brian Keith

- 1960—*Gold of the Seven Saints*, with Clint Walker, Roger Moore, and Chill Wills

- 1961—*The Comancheros*, with John Wayne, Lee Marvin, and Shirley Jones

- 1963—*The Greatest Story Ever Told*, with Max Von Sydow, and Carrol Baker

- 1963—*Cheyenne Autumn*, with Richard Widmark, Carol Baker, and Karl Malden

- 1964—*Rio Conchos*, with Richard Boone and Stewart Whitman

- 1966—*Wild Rovers*, with William Holden and Ryan O'Neal

- 1967—*Fade Inn*, with Burt Reynolds and Barbara Loden

- 1967—*Blue*, with Terrence Stamp, Ricardo Montalban, and Karl Malden

- 1972—*Alias Smith and Jones* (for television), with Ben Murphy and Roger Davis

- 1975—*Against a Crooked Sky*, with Richard Boone

- 1982—*Space Hunter—Adventure in the Forbidden Zone*, with Peter Strauss

- 1984—*Choke Canyon*, with Steve Collins and Janet Julian

- 1988—*Indiana Jones and the Last Crusade*, with Harrison Ford and Sean Connery

- 1990—*Thelma and Louise*, with Susan Sarandon and Geena Davis

- 1993—*Geronimo*, with Robert Duval

- 1994—*City Slickers II*, with Billy Crystal and Jack Palance

- 1996—*Breakdown*, with Kurt Russell, J.T. Walsh, and Kathleen Quinlan

- 1999—*Galaxy Quest*, with Tim Allen and Sigourney Weaver

- 2000—*Mission Impossible 2*, with Tom Cruise

- 2002—*Goldmember*, with Austin Powers

- 2003—*The Book of Mormon Movie, Volume I*

- 2005—*Don't Come Knocking*, with Jessica Lange

Originally, the Moab landscape was synonymous with Westerns, and it was hard to break the mold. But in later years, Moab became the backdrop for otherworldly adventures in outer space, and offered the wide-open spaces sought by fugitives Thelma and Louise. Nearby Lake Powell was the *Planet of the Apes*.

The movie industry has had an on-again-off-again relationship with Moab. There have been periods of feast and famine. The films were an economic boon to the area in the early 1950s, when the economy was depressed and people were out of work. The production companies hired many of the locals as extras, as workers around the sets, or to handle livestock and logistics. But by the early 1960s, Moab's population had increased fivefold in the wake of the Uranium Boom, and the movie industry was not as big a deal. Everyone had good jobs in the mining industry, and Grand County had one of the highest per-capita income levels in Utah. Even though eight major features were filmed in Moab during the 1960s, the community was less dependent on the film industry for economic reasons. It was a good thing, too, for Hollywood began to show less interest in the 1970s and '80s.

There were several reasons that fewer films were made in the area after 1970. Television took a big bite of the movie industry, and a flood of foreign films competed for moviegoer dollars. Fewer and fewer movies were filmed on location in an effort to cut costs. Another factor was increased regulation by the Bureau of Land Management and the National Parks Service. In the early days, there were no national parks in the area, and no permits were required to use the public lands for anything. By the 1970s and '80s, strict guidelines were in place that made movie companies responsible for ecological damage, trash, and tracks. While a good idea that was long overdue, the requirements made filming more expensive.

There was a small rebound in the 1990s, and interest has continued through today. However, much of today's film work is in TV

**Filming in the Park Avenue section of Court House Towers in
Arches National Park, 1960
(Museum of Moab photo NN-5)**

programming, commercials, TV specials, documentaries, and even
pop music videos. The famous TV commercials in which a new car is
perched on top of a slender spire of rock high above a scenic desert
landscape were filmed near Moab. The slender rock spire is Castle
Rock in nearby Castle Valley.

The new film productions are considerably smaller than the epic,
big-screen projects of the 1950s and '60s, and not as important to
Moab's economy. Most movies today are filmed in studios with the
scenery supplied by electronic wizardry. But even now, it is not a surprise when Moabites spot a familiar landmark used as a backdrop for
movies, television shows, or commercials.

The Moab Film Commission has changed over the years, too.
For a few years, the commission was linked with other areas of
southern Utah and known as the "Moab to Monument Valley Film

Commission." But more recently, Grand County discontinued funding the film commission, and the entire venture wilted and died. Moab's close relationship with Hollywood is now a thing of the past. Times change.

But whatever the story or the imagined location, there is no backdrop for a film more spectacular than Moab's backyard. No other place on earth is more photogenic.

The World's Most Scenic
Garbage Dump

In 1986 the Moab Chamber of Commerce was brainstorming ways to attract tourists to the area. While discussing the scenic attractions, a comment was made that even the Moab city dump was in a setting of scenic splendor unmatched by any other

The world's most scenic garbage dump—center right (author photo)

town. Carrying that thought a little further down the trail, the chamber decided to hold a "World's Most Scenic Garbage Dump" contest. It would be a great way to have a little fun while promoting the town.

The contest turned out to be a gem of marketing genius. The idea caught the imagination of the whole country, and the promotion created publicity the chamber had never dreamed of. Within weeks, newspapers from all over the world were running stories about the contest. The Moab Chamber of Commerce was flooded with calls, letters, and requests for information. Tourists began stopping in town to ask directions to the garbage dump. For a few years, the city landfill might have been the most visited and the most photographed site in Grand County.

But the official contest ended in a tie. Moab officials had to admit that Kodiak, Alaska, had a garbage dump as scenic as their own. In a fine spirit of good sportsmanship, Moab agreed to share the "World's Most Scenic Dump" honors with the City of Kodiak. In fact, the two towns became "sister cities" because of the contest.

H-Bomb at Church Rock?

I n the early evening of January 19, 1961, the sky south of Moab suddenly lit up with a brilliant flash of fire, and a thunderous roar split the silence. A huge B-52 bomber exploded in mid-air and came raining down over the desert in a thousand flaming pieces. Incredibly, few people witnessed the event. It was a cold winter night, the area was sparsely inhabited, and most people from the surrounding small towns and farms were indoors. The point of impact was slightly east of Highway 191, about forty miles south of Moab, near Church Rock and the road junction to Canyonlands National Park.

The Stratofortress was on the first leg of a training flight that would have taken her in a wide arc over the intermountain west, to South Dakota, and then back to her point of origin at Briggs Air Force Base near El Paso, Texas. The big plane was flying at about forty thousand feet when she encountered violent turbulence that caused her to roll over and fall several thousand feet. As the heavy bomber tumbled toward the ground, she went into a vertical spin and began to break apart. The left wing caught fire, and fuel tanks exploded at an altitude of about seven thousand feet.

Incredibly, three members of the seven-man crew were able to bail out. When law officers and passersby from the nearby highway arrived at the scene shortly after the crash, they found two members of the crew—the co-pilot and the navigator—walking around amid the flaming wreckage. Both men were stunned but not seriously injured. They both reported seeing a third parachute descending near the wreckage. Within a short time, law officers from San Juan and Grand counties were able to put more than one hundred volunteers into the area to search for the missing parachutist. The search continued into the early morning hours. Four bodies were found and identified in the wreckage, but the missing man, eventually identified as the flight engineer, was not found.

Air Force personnel from Utah's Hill Air Force Base were on the scene within a few hours and took charge of the investigation. Almost immediately, all civilians were ordered away from the crash site. The highway was closed for a time, and a large area was evacuated, much to the consternation of some of the locals. An Air Force Colonel gave a public statement saying that the military didn't know if the plane was carrying any bombs or classified materials. It was a ludicrous pronouncement. Surely the Air Force knew what the bomber's mission was and what was on board.

Finally, on the morning of January 21, a full thirty-six hours after the crash, the San Juan County search-and-rescue teams were allowed to resume the search for the missing flight engineer. They found the man within an hour, not far from the crash site. He had survived the mid-air explosion and a parachute landing in the dark, but had frozen to death while waiting to be rescued. He was found under a pinyon tree, wrapped in his parachute in an attempt to stay warm. He had been dead only a few hours when found.

There has been a good deal of speculation over the years that the B-52 might have been carrying nuclear weapons when she fell from the sky. Why was the colonel less than honest in his public statement? Why were rescue teams ordered out of the area while a crewmember was still listed as missing? What was removed from the crash site?

And those who suspected nuclear weapons at the scene might have been proven right. In the early 1990s, a study commissioned by the U.S. Senate listed the eastern Utah B-52 crash as one of twenty-nine possible nuclear weapons accidents since the beginning of the Cold War. However, the official Air Force story, to this day, is that no atomic weapons were aboard the aircraft. Who knows? Church Rock and the Land of Moab might have survived a close call.

Murder and Mystery

It was the biggest manhunt ever conducted by law enforcement officers anywhere in southeastern Utah. Dozens of law officers and FBI agents, along with many dozens of ordinary citizens, both armed and unarmed, beat the bushes of Grand County for three days and nights in July 1961. The ground search was supplemented by several boats on the river, fixed-wing aircraft, and five navy helicopters lent to the search by government officials doing an aerial survey of the proposed Canyonlands National Park. The object of the search was a missing 15-year-old girl, Denise Sullivan, and the man who had killed her mother, shot a family friend, and kidnapped Denise.

The incident happened on the road just outside of Dead Horse Point State Park on the evening of July 4, 1961. Three tourists from Connecticut—55-year-old Charles Boothroyd, 41-year-old Jeanette Sullivan, and Sullivan's 15-year-old daughter, Denise—were visiting Utah and decided to stop and see the newly created state park at Dead Horse Point. The park was only two years old that summer, and there was only one ranger to oversee the whole place. The area was fairly isolated, and there were few visitors.

Boothroyd and the Sullivans enjoyed the afternoon at Dead Horse Point. While there, they were befriended by a smiling stranger who volunteered to show them the sights. They spent a couple of hours with the man, who told them stories and seemed to know the area well.

When the visitors left the park late that afternoon, they found their self-appointed tour guide parked alongside the road with the hood of his car up, as if he was having car trouble. The group stopped to see if they could be of some assistance. But when Boothroyd and Mrs. Sullivan got out of the car, the man came at them with a .22 rifle and demanded all of their money. Mrs. Sullivan resisted and was shot in the head and killed. Boothroyd was shot twice in the face, but miraculously survived. Denise was kidnapped.

Within a few minutes, an oilfield worker who had heard the shooting came to investigate and found Boothroyd bleeding but still conscious at the edge of the road. By two-way radio, the oil worker sounded the alarm. Boothroyd was able to give a description of both the murderer and his automobile. An immediate manhunt was begun, and the FBI was notified.

For three days and three nights, the whole area was under siege. Law officers and citizens patrolled the roads and canyons, airplanes and helicopters buzzed the mesas, and watercraft patrolled the river canyons, looking for the car, the suspect, and his young victim. It was about ten P.M. on July 7 when FBI agents stopped a car matching the suspect vehicle headed north on the highway toward Crescent Junction. When federal agents confronted the driver, he pulled a  pistol and shot himself in the head. He died a few hours later at the hospital in Moab.

The man was Abel Aragon, an unemployed coalminer from nearby Carbon County, Utah. Aragon was a highly decorated ex-Marine, a recipient of the Navy Cross and Purple Heart in World War II. He had been in the Moab area for a week or two looking for work and had spent some time at Polar Mesa, a mining camp on the slopes of the La Sal Mountains. At the mining camp, law officers found the rifle used to commit the crime and other evidence, but teenaged Denise Sullivan was never found.

Officers dragged the river for her body and searched the canyons and overlooks for weeks, but to no avail. The case remains, to this day, one of the most heinous, troubling, and unsolved missing-persons mysteries in the Land of Moab.

The Rocket's Red Glare

I n the 1960s and 1970s, Moab was "downrange" in the Cold War—literally. Hundreds of ballistic missiles were fired over the town. Of course, in the interests of safety, none of the missiles were supposed to go directly "over" the town. But to rockets flying at supersonic speeds on the fringes of outer space, twenty or thirty miles is close enough for government work.

It all started in 1963, when the army established the Utah Launch Complex near the town of Green River, about sixty miles northwest of Moab. The site was chosen as a test site for rocket research using Athena rockets, and for the development of the Pershing nuclear missile. The Pershing was designed for use by NATO armies in Europe as a medium-range tactical battlefield weapon.

Over the next twelve years, hundreds of Athena and Pershing rockets were fired from Green River to White Sands Missile Range in southern New Mexico, almost five hundred miles away. A smaller, temporary launch site was also set up on Black Mesa near Blanding, Utah. The Black Mesa site was used to test mobile Pershing rocket launchers. The reasoning behind the domestic, in-our-backyard testing was to keep results secret from the Russians. Russian fishing vessels with lots of antennae had been shadowing American missile tests in the Pacific Ocean for years.

the Utah to New Mexico missile testing was the first time that ballistic missiles were fired over populated areas of the United States—and, hopefully, it will be the only time. The flight path covered one of the most sparsely settled regions of the country, but the missiles still flew over, or near, several small towns, three Indian reservations, several major highways, and Canyonlands National Park.

The test flights were unpredictable and dangerous, even though test rockets were not armed with real warheads. People in the direct line of fire—rural farm families, Utes, Navajos, cowboys, uranium miners, and tourists—were evacuated before each missile test. Evacuees who had to leave their homes and livelihoods were paid a per diem and mileage for the inconvenience. Tourists and travelers were not. Moab and other small towns were never evacuated, because the missiles were not supposed to pass directly overhead.

There was good reason for the evacuations that did occur. The rockets were multi-stage, and big chunks would come crashing down helter-skelter out over the landscape as each section burned out. Helicopters scurried about over the desert, collecting the fragments as they fell.

And more than a few missiles went off course and had to be destroyed in the air, an event that sent showering debris over a wide area. A few others went astray before they could be destroyed, some landing in strange and unexpected places. The very first Athena rocket fired from Green River missed its mark by 250 miles and landed near Durango, Colorado, causing some consternation amongst the good citizens. Another Athena launched later the same year was destroyed in the air, with big chunks landing just five miles outside of Blanding, Utah. In 1969, a Pershing missile, destroyed in the air, came crashing down seven miles east of the town of Bluff, Utah. And then, in 1970, another Pershing overshot the intended target area and went whistling into Old Mexico, sparking an international incident.

The Utah Launch Complex was closed in 1975 after shooting 448 missiles into southern New Mexico and other unintended points along the way. The test program helped to develop and perfect America's front-line tactical missile system during the Cold War, and thousands of U.S. and NATO troops were trained at the Utah launch sites. The shell of an Athena missile is on display in the Green River City Park.

The army tried to reopen the Green River Launch Complex in 1982, but a lot had changed in seven years. The idea sparked a great deal of opposition. Tourism was a big deal in southern Utah by then. The state and its impacted communities were not happy to anticipate frequent evacuations and road closings to accommodate the launches. Environmental groups protested vigorously, and even Utah's governor was against renewed missile testing over the canyon country. The new rocket plan was shot down.

To date, the Green River missile complex has not reopened and probably never will. The night sky around Moab is a friendly place today. What appear to be bottle rockets zipping through the stars are meteorites and not ballistic missiles.

The Mother Of All Bombs

After Moab became internationally famous as a tourist destination, a few products were named in honor of the town. In the 1990s, the Schwinn bicycle company began manufacturing a "Moab model" mountain bike, and Nike put out a "Mowabb" hiking shoe. The Asolo Company also manufactures a "Moab XCR hiking shoe" for men.

But when the United States military got into the act, the city of Moab protested. In 2003 the Air Force tested the first GBU-43/B Massive Ordinance Air Blast Bomb. The MOABB is the largest-ever "satellite guided, air-delivered weapon in history." The bomb is 30 feet long, 40.5 inches in diameter, and weighs 21,700 pounds. Because of its size and weight, the bomb is dropped from a C-130 cargo plane on a parachute skid and not from a bomber. Needless to say, the eleven-ton monster makes a big splash when detonated. The MOABB was rushed into production for use in Afghanistan and Iraq.

Moab city officials asked government officials to change the name of the bomb when newspapers and magazines began using a slang term that service members were using for the weapon. The military people were calling it the "Mother Of All Bombs" and using the acronym "MOAB," without the final "B." But, as could be predicted in the bomb-making business, the petition from Moab's city fathers fell on deaf ears. The bomb is still known as the MOAB.

Marijuana Mesa

On Tuesday night, February 15, 1983, at about ten P.M., a twin-engine Piper aircraft crashed about five miles south of the Canyonlands Airport. The pilot hadn't filed a flight plan, and no one knew about the crash until a Russian satellite picked up signals from the plane's emergency locator beacon and relayed the information to the U.S. State Department. After an investigation, the National Transportation Safety Board (NTSB) determined the plane had been flying at an altitude of 5,359 feet when it encountered a rocky mesa top with a height of 5,500 feet. Not good. The weather was clear, but the night was very dark, and the pilot was legally drunk and tested positive for drugs. Two people were killed in the crash and debris was scattered for one hundred yards across the top of the mesa.

The crash site was in rugged country without a road or easy access on foot. When sheriffs' deputies got to the scene the next morning in a helicopter, they found the dead pilot and passenger and one thousand pounds of marijuana scattered around the crash site. They were able to recover about eight hundred pounds, which was burned, but an estimated two hundred pounds more was deemed unrecoverable, as the packaging had ripped open and the killer weed was scattered all over the crash site.

There are rumors that a few weeks after the plane crash, some people in Moab were happily lighting up what was called PCP at the time, an acronym that stood for Plane Crash Pot. It is said that PCP was easily identifiable because of red sand, juniper twigs, and other foreign materials mixed in with the "good stuff." Supposedly a few hardy souls had hiked to the remote crash site and meticulously "salvaged" what was left of the illegal cargo. It was even suggested that law officers might have overlooked a few intact bags that were thrown from the plane on impact. Whatever the truth of the rumor, some locals still refer to the crash site as Marijuana Mesa.

* * *

Something in the Water?

Who wants to drink water that is forty years old? And yet, turn a tap in Moab and that's exactly what you get. The water that fills your glass in 2007 went into the system in 1967. That's right. Moab city water is as old as Julia Roberts.

You see, there is an underground aquifer—a thick layer of porous rock that slowly filters Moab water into the municipal water system. Water enters the aquifer upstream as melted snow and rainwater, then spends forty years seeping through the natural stone filter before entering the well and ultimately the tap. It's nature's handiwork at its finest and a great source of pure, clean water.

However, questions do arise from time to time about strange behaviors and weird moods that sometimes affect people who linger in the community. Could it be something in the water?

Let's see ... people who were running around Moab with Geiger counters in the 1950s were drinking water that went into the system around 1910, when Madame Curie was doing experiments with radon. Kids in Moab who danced the Twist, the Watusi, and the Mashed Potato in the 1960s were drinking water that entered the system during the "flapper" dance craze of the 1920s. People who celebrated the first "Earth Day" at Moab in 1970 were drinking water that went into the system in 1930, the year the world fell apart on Wall Street. The first tourists to bring bicycles to Moab in the early 1980s were drinking water that went into the system in the early 1940s, when everyone had to park their cars because of wartime gas rationing. People who protested the radioactive tailings pile near Moab in the 1990s were drinking water that went into the system in the 1950s, the years Moab became "The Uranium Capital of the World."

So in 2009 people will be drinking water that entered the system in 1969, the year Woodstock—the greatest single gathering of hippie flower children during the "love-in" days of the 1960s—made the front pages. If the theory holds true, 2009 might be a "groovy" year in Moab.

Wilderness for
Fun and Profit

In their letters and journals, the first settlers of Moab spoke of the natural beauty of the landscape. They were impressed by the scenery, but they saw the land from a different perspective than we view it today. Many of their writings use adjectives like barren, wild, desolate, bleak, broken, and forlorn. Eastern Utah really was wilderness in those days, and it was not a friendly place.

Wilderness in the 1800s was a place to fear and avoid. Only the bravest of people went there, and when they did, they went well prepared. People traveled in groups and carried guns for protection. Wilderness was a place of trouble, a blank spot on the map that served as a hideout for outlaws and outcasts. Murderers, thieves, and roving bands of wild Indians haunted the canyons. The land was also filled with dangerous animals. Wolves, bears, cougars, and coyotes were a threat to people and the livestock they depended on for transportation and survival. There were no medical facilities, and a broken bone, a summer chill, or an infected tooth could be life threatening.

The land itself was dangerous. River crossings were a nightmare, and the muddy water took a heavy toll of people, livestock, and equipment. People died from exposure to the elements. Heat stroke, frostbite, and hypothermia were common among wilderness travelers, depending on the time of year. There were flash floods in the canyons, quicksand, cactus, and poisonous plants, bugs, snakes, and water. There was seldom any help when people got into any kind of trouble. Travelers were on their own, live or die.

Thankfully, times have changed. The red desert of today is the same place the pioneers wrote about, but it is different now—it is a friendly wilderness. Gone are the outlaws, wild Indians, most of the dangerous animals, the hazards of the trail, and the sense of true isolation. There are good roads, bridges, towns, phone towers, airplanes, and satellites now. There is always a park ranger, a highway patrol officer, or a search-and-rescue team in a helicopter just a cell phone call away. The lower forty-eight states have no true wilderness anymore, even though many thousands of acres have been set aside as "wilderness" or "wilderness study areas." The Elk Mountain Missionaries of 1855 would laugh at what we call wilderness.

> People did not travel for fun or just to see the sights during the days of true wilderness. Travel was hard work and serious business.

Wilderness today is a state of mind. We imagine the experience more than we partake of the reality. Never having known true wilderness, we often confuse it with open spaces. What most people mean today when they speak of wilderness is a place where they can breathe clean air and be alone for a time in beautiful, rugged country. They really don't want true wilderness, with the inherent dangers, hardships, and uncertainties. If they did, they would flock to places like the Amazon, Antarctica, or Mount Everest. What they really want is "wilderness" that is easy accessible, with good roads, trails, signs, maps, toilets, and rescue helicopters standing by. If this were not the case, our national parks would be empty.

The wilderness most people seek today is simply a quiet and semi-remote place to escape the hubbub of the city and the pressures of a high-stress job. They want wilderness to be a lovely park where a person can commune with nature and find freedom from the ticking minutes of a hectic schedule and the clutter of technology. It is a worthy dream. Friendly wilderness, Garden-of-Eden wilderness, is something many people spend their lives searching for. Some might say the dream takes us back to our roots and fulfills an inherent longing in the human psyche.

And because it is something that everybody wants, we sell it. We promote it, package it, and market it like any other commodity. Thousands of people make their living in the wilderness business. Tour guides, river runners, people who sell jeeps, bikes, and ATVs, outdoor supply houses, sporting goods manufacturers, publishers, photographers, airplane pilots, government workers, cops, cooks, convenience store clerks, search-and-rescue teams, and even some lawyers and advocates all owe their livelihoods to the business of wilderness. It has become a multi-billion dollar industry and a fine example of capitalism at its best. Jobs are created, fortunes and reputations made, goods produced, services provided, and money exchanged. Tourism provides a lot of jobs and a good tax base for places like Moab and the State of Utah.

Wilderness for fun and profit—that's what the southern Utah tourist business is all about, like it or not. It's an important business, too. People need wilderness. Wilderness can be physically demanding and spiritually uplifting. We need the open space, clean air, and feeling of isolation, even if it's only a perception.

The days of the old West are gone—and good riddance. What we have today is better than the old West. We have good roads today on which we can travel freely without being attacked by bandits or bears. We don't have to worry about being gut shot with an arrow or kicked in the head by a stupid horse. We can roll up the windows and enjoy air conditioning if we don't want to eat dust or be tortured by gnats. We can cross the river on a bridge at fifty miles an hour and not even see the water if we don't want to turn our heads. We can sleep out under the stars without worrying about being captured by slave traders or having wolves kill our horses, leaving us stranded one hundred miles from anywhere. We can stop at a fast food joint when we get hungry

We go winging over the slickrock on soft rubber tires with bike spokes singing in the wind and a warm, friendly sun caressing our back. We worry only about the steepness of the next hill, the depth of the next sand bog, and where to choose to eat when the sun goes down and we drift back into the lights of town.

If they could only see us now, the covered-wagon pioneers would be envious. And those tough frontier women might sit down and cry. We are lucky people and greatly blessed. Daniel Boone can keep the wilderness of yesterday. Modern wilderness is better.

instead of taking an hour to kindle a fire alongside the road and peel potatoes. There is food, water, shelter, medical help, and entertainment in abundance along the fringes of the modern wilderness, and we are free to partake. Gone are the days of traveling with fear, cold, and hunger. We can enjoy the journey, something our forefathers never imagined.

A Day in the Desert

The first rays of morning light sweep over the canyon rim. Sandstone responds with a warm, orange glow. Where only moments before the earth was dark with shadow, it now comes alive with brilliant color. Red dirt, purple sage, and straw-colored grass blend with ocean waves of rusted stone. There is no audible sound, and yet you can hear, or maybe just feel, the world coming to life in the cool morning air. As the sun draws colors from the shadows, it lights everything it touches with the fire of life. A new day is born in the canyon country.

There is depth to the landscape. Ridges and hills, mesas and canyons, sand flats, bluffs, and far-away mountains take shape in the gathering light. It is endless country, empty and quiet, hushed in the dawning and the promise of the new day. Far-off mountain peaks shine in the morning light. Snow glistens and sparkles. A soft blanket of timber hangs down on the slopes.

The edge of the sky becomes ragged and rough as the sun sweeps across the valley, pushing back shadows and revealing the land. A city of stone emerges on the far horizon. Castles and spires reach into the sky. There are battlements, minarets, shaded windows, and draw-bridges like those in a land of fairytales. Turrets, walls, and watchtowers shine in the sun like the fabled El Dorado, the lost city

Temple Mountain on the San Raphael Swell

of gold. Soldiers guard the approaches, misshapen ogres with otherworldly proportions, hoodoos and goblins of soft, weathered stone.

By noontime the sand is hot and the sun bores down. Bright light fades the auburn slick-rock to the color of faded burlap. The smooth stone reflects the desert sun, and dark glasses tint the landscape with a pale shade of gray. Tiny tracks of bugs, birds, lizards, and mice are etched onto the smooth, wind-blown sand with exotic patterns that twist, swirl, and wander. Native sunflowers stand with drooping heads, wilted, up to their knees in the hot, drifting sand.

The desert is filled with exotic smells rising on thermal currents of midday air. The hot sun draws sap from the pinyon trees and opens the pores of sage leaves, prickly pear, wild flowers, and weeds. There is the perfume of sage, an aromatic hint of desert juniper, the tart fragrance of pinyon pine, the sour scent of rabbit brush, and the stink of hot alkali mud in the bottom of a shallow creek bed. Chew a needle of pinyon to experience the taste of wilderness. Walk a sand dune barefoot to be a kid again.

Shade is pleasant in the shadow of a canyon wall. Coolness envelops you like a blanket after a long hike in the merciless sun. Voices echo in the shadow of the ledges and people speak with hushed and muted tones. It's like being in a cathedral—every sound echoes, and your eyes are drawn upward by the massive stone walls towering high overhead. Far above, red sandstone meets a cobalt blue sky where tufts of cotton clouds drift silently by.

A sparrow hawk disrupts the silence with a trilling cry that reverberates through the canyon. The sound grabs your attention and you instantly look up, searching for the falcon along the face of the cliff. When you finally spot him, you are amazed by how small he is compared to the big noise he makes. The little hawk with the big voice sails slowly overhead at the very top of the canyon wall, riding warm thermal air currents with wings outstretched, shining in the sun like a paper kite.

A walk along the canyon wall reveals a petroglyph panel, an aboriginal signpost many centuries old. A string of small desert sheep pose proudly, while a hopeful human with bow and arrow takes aim. The carving is old, weathered, and partly faded.

By late afternoon, the sky is changing. The light has softened and shadows are growing long. A quiet calm permeates everything. The smallest sounds travel for miles and miles, amplified by the ledges and canyon walls. Ravens wing homeward, flying low over the dunes, calling to each other as they fly, talking over the events of the day. Ragged fingers of night slowly pull a blanket of shade over the valley floor, fading colors to gray and putting day-creatures to bed. Soon it will be dark.

The setting sun sets the sky on fire. Clouds burn with fiery red and florescent orange. Bright blades of golden light reach from the horizon and keep the cloud fires lit as the sun slips ever lower behind the rim. Reflected light bathes the desert in a pale shade of pink. A misty haze seems to fill the valley. Snowcaps on distant mountain peaks glisten pink, orange, and blue, and then the sun is gone and the mountain fades into purple darkness.

the ancient rock art poses many questions. Did the arrow find its mark? Was the man who carved the panel bragging or praying? How many years has it been since this time capsule was carved? How many people have seen it in the years since? How much longer will it last before wind and rain reduce it to dust?

Night on the desert and the world is alive. Crickets sing and nighthawks swoop through the dark sky, scooping up bugs and sounding their "whooshing" radar-like calls. Bats zip through the air—clumsily, comically, even recklessly—performing impossible feats of short-winged aerobatics. Far across the valley a coyote sings his nightly song—a couple of cheerful yips followed by a mournful howl. His lady friend answers, surprisingly close, and you wonder if she's been watching as you prepare your camp.

The night gets darker and stars appear like a heavenly carpet of tiny Christmas lights. They sparkle and gleam with tints of red, yellow, and blue. Silently, a full moon appears over the eastern horizon, a single, shining coin in the night sky, a buffed and polished quarter at first, and then a silver dime as it moves higher, away from the mountain. The brightness of the moon dims the starlight to a softer tone, and a quiet peacefulness fills the night air. Moonlight washes down over the desert. Rock spires, juniper trees, canyons, and ledges are bathed in the soft night light that reveals smooth waves of stone on a dark ocean of sand and sage that stretches endlessly toward the midnight blue horizon.

Far away in the darkness, small dots of light move silently through the night, a reminder that civilization and the interstate highway are not so very far away. The thought is comforting. Neanderthals and Eskimos have known true wilderness, and they can keep it all. The distant car lights shimmer and fade on the dark horizon, and then they disappear.

From the quiet calm of a sleeping bag, the night sky appears to be a busy place. Satellites scoot through the darkness in severely straight lines. It seems amazing they never bump into the stars. Meteorites with long tails of white sparks zip silently across the heavens. Airliners plod along slowly, winking lights on the tips of their wings. The growl and rumble of jet engines has become a normal part of the desert night and doesn't seem an intrusion anymore. Far off on the mesa top, an owl calls out, the sound echoing softly as it floats away in the blackness.

Slowly you fade into the world of dreams—peaceful sleep in the cool, desert air. Angels of the desert watch over you as you rest. You are in the bosom of Mother Nature as she cradles you like a child.

The Secret Name of a Utah State Treasure

Arches National Park is one of the best-known tourist destinations in the United States, and one of the most popular sites to see in Arches is Delicate Arch. Delicate Arch is truly awe-inspiring, and hundreds of thousands of people have made the pilgrimage up the steep access trail to view the sandstone wonder. The scenery is worth the hike.

For many years, Delicate Arch has been an official emblem of the State of Utah. The image is found on letterheads, logos, and Utah state license plates. It can also be found on an endless variety of tourist trade goods, from spoons and refrigerator magnets to coffee mugs, T-shirts, and anything in between. Everyone knows Delicate Arch.

What a lot of people don't know is that the name "Delicate Arch" is a fairly recent moniker. In fact, the old cowboys would laugh if they could see the image in all the places we

Delicate Arch—known to old cowboys
as the Schoolmarm's Bloomers
(author photo)

find it today. For you see, Delicate Arch wasn't Delicate Arch until after the place was designated a national monument and required some "taming" to make it more suitable to share with the rest of the world. To the old cowboys around Moab, Delicate Arch was known as "The Schoolmarm's Bloomers."

A Red-Rock Field of Dreams

Moab is the most beautiful country in the world, but it has always struggled to sustain economic growth. For many years the economy was rooted in farming and ranching. These are noble professions, but they do not employ large numbers of people. And it takes a lot of land to make a living off the land. There is often no room for the next generation. For more than one hundred years, the major export for many of Utah's small, rural farming communities has been the children. Moab is no exception.

As Moab entered the early years of the twentieth century, the younger generation found that all of the good places for farms and ranches had already been taken. Mining and milling were able to employ some of the sons and grandsons of pioneers, especially during the days of the Uranium Boom of the 1950s, but the mining industry is unpredictable. Too often mining creates a boom-and-bust economy—things go great for a while and then tank for a variety of reasons, only to resurge again in ten or twenty years. A stable, more diversified economy is better.

With an ever-expanding population and only limited opportunities for economic growth and development, some of Moab's city fathers recognized early that the town's future might be in the tourist business. There was no place anywhere with greater tourist potential than Moab. The town had the world's finest scenery, the healthiest climate, and much-heralded scenic wonders. John Wesley Powell had extolled the beauty and the virtues of the canyon country in his popular books and writings as early as the 1870s. *National Geographic* had published articles about the scenic marvels of southern Utah by 1906, and Teddy Roosevelt had officially proclaimed Natural Bridges, 120 miles south of Moab, as Utah's first national monument in 1908. But few people had ever visited the area. All the Moab city fathers had to do was convince people to come and see what was in their backyard—and provide a way for them to get there.

But in the early days of Moab, the town was an island of tourism potential on an ocean of inaccessibility. Roads were crude, and the town was hard to get to. And while the railroad was relatively close, it was still difficult to transport freight and passengers those last thirty-five miles to Moab in horse-drawn wagons and coaches. The trip took two days for a freight wagon, and conditions were primitive. To people reared in the eastern states, where rivers and canals were a primary means of transportation, the solution seemed obvious. The Green and Colorado rivers were waiting to become major transportation corridors for the whole region.

There was a possible water link between Moab and the railroad, too. The railroad crossed the Green River at the town of Green River, about sixty miles northwest of Moab. If freight and passengers could be offloaded at the rail depot there, they could be floated down the Green to the confluence of the Colorado and then paddled up that river all the way to Moab. The water route would cover almost two hundred miles, but some thought it would be more practical and more comfortable than the thirty-five-mile, sand-and-mud-bogged wagon road in use at the time. People should be able to travel the water route in relative luxury and ease, enjoying the scenery and arriving in Moab happy, clean, and in good spirits after the journey.

The first riverboat to attempt the route was called the *Major Powell*, in honor of John Wesley Powell, the famous river explorer of the 1860s and '70s. The *Major Powell*, launched in 1891, was a rather humble, thirty-five-foot craft sporting a small, wood-burning steam

The Colorado River steamboat *Undine* in 1902, shortly before she sank
(Museum of Moab photo VS-5)

engine with twin screws. She began her maiden voyage down the
Green River with much fanfare, but hit a rock and bent her propellers
only seven miles below her starting point.

It took a year to fix the *Major Powell*, but in 1892, she began the
journey again. The second time she was successful, but the 370-mile
round trip took all of two weeks, and the boat was found to be woe-
fully underpowered. She never made the trip again.

The next venture was in 1902, when a fifty-six-foot paddleboat
called the *Undine* took to the river. The *Undine* had a 20-horsepower,
coal-fired steam engine, a shallow draft, and adequate power, and she
made the first trip to Moab without any recorded difficulties. But
after reaching Moab, her captain decided to see how far up the river
he could take her. He might have had his sights set on establishing
another riverboat landing somewhere closer to Grand Junction,
Colorado. Unfortunately, while negotiating a rapid, the *Undine* powered out, turned sideways to the current, and capsized. Everyone on
board was rescued, but the boat was lost.

The next year, a very small, twenty-seven-foot side-wheeled paddleboat called the *Wilmont* took to the river with a new-fangled 7.5 horsepower gasoline engine. The *Wilmont* made a couple of successful trips between Green River and Moab, but she was too small to carry enough cargo and passengers to make a profit. Her service was discontinued after those two trips.

In 1905 the Green River and Moab Navigation Company was formed, and the partners intended to get into the riverboat business in a big way. They launched a fine fifty-five-foot boat called the *City of Moab*. The boat was a high-profile double-decker with "luxurious accommodations." She was twin-propped and powered by two thirty-horsepower gasoline engines, and she would have looked right at home on the Mississippi. The days of high-class river boating had finally arrived in eastern Utah.

Unfortunately, the *City of Moab* drank a lot of gasoline, which was a rare commodity in southeastern Utah in 1905. In May of that year, on her first trip, her tanks went dry pushing against the high-water current of the Colorado. When her engines sputtered to a stop a few miles below Moab, the boat washed back downstream and was wrecked against the shore. Luckily, no one was hurt.

The *City of Moab* was repaired and refueled, and then started back to Green River, giving up on the high-water current of the Colorado. Unfortunately, the Green River was running a lot of water, too, and the big boat ran out of gas a second time. She had to be beached and tied to a sandbar a few miles below the town of Green River.

After her humiliating maiden voyage, the *City of Moab* was reconfigured to a sternwheeler, and her "luxuries" and weight were downsized to make her lighter and more seaworthy. She was renamed the *Cliff Dweller* to give her a new start in life, but bad luck was still her main cargo. She still couldn't pull the swift currents and kept running aground on sandbars. Finally, the bad luck boat was sold to a company who shipped her to the Great Salt Lake to be used as a tour boat named the *Vista*. She had better luck chugging through the flat salt brine of Utah's Dead Sea.

In 1907 another paddlewheeler called the *Black Eagle* blew up on her maiden voyage before reaching Moab. She had a water-tube steam engine that clogged with silt, sending her boiler pressures off the clock. By a miracle, no one was reported killed or seriously injured in the explosion.

Finally, in 1909, the Army Corps of Engineers did a formal navigational study of the river route between Green River and Moab and determined that the waterway was not suitable as a commercial route. The study ended any hope some might have had of securing funding for future projects. Local businessmen were sorely disappointed.

In the 1920s and '30s, the Moab Garage Company ran a series of small craft up and down the rivers, delivering supplies, passengers, and spare parts to mines and oil drilling operations. The small-scale riverboat venture was quite successful, and the company made money for as long as the mines and drill rigs were in business.

But the dream of a big paddlewheel boat plying the river with banjos playing and happy tourists smiling just wouldn't die. In 1972 Tex McClatchy launched a big sternwheeler aimed at giving Moab tourists a grand tour of the river canyons in luxury and style. The boat was christened the *Canyon King*, but it was quickly apparent that the river, and not the boat, was still the king of the canyons. The new boat had a tough time navigating the constantly fluctuating water level of the Colorado, and she kept running aground on the shifting sandbars. The boat was finally shipped to Lake Powell, where she could float free and proud in deeper water. The *Canyon King* is now a floating restaurant at the Wahweep Marina near the Glen Canyon Dam.

The 185-mile Green River to Moab water route was not completely abandoned. In the late 1960s, it became the path for an annual Easter weekend boat outing called the "Friendship Cruise." The yearly event was enjoyed by hundreds of people piloting dozens of small, privately owned pleasure boats. Unfortunately, the event was discontinued in 2004 and might never be held again.

Tex McClatchy's *Canyon King* at the time of her maiden voyage in 1972
(Museum of Moab photo)

After the riverboat ventures all went under, it was the Denver and Rio Grande Western Railroad that promised hope for creating a tourist industry for Moab. The railroad offered the fastest and easiest access to all of eastern Utah in those days when roads were primitive and horsepower really was the power of a horse. The D&RGW line between Denver and Salt Lake City was completed in 1883, and Thompson Springs, about thirty-five miles north of Moab, became an important stop. The railroad was a lifeline that made the development of eastern Utah possible. Freight, livestock, and people crowded the train depot at Thompson Springs.

In 1923 Alexander Ringhoffer met with railroad officials and took them to see what would soon become Arches National Monument. The railroad people were excited about the possibility of transporting lots of tourists to the area, and they helped to promote the idea and get the area nominated as a national monument. But in spite of some hopeful advertising, tourists didn't come to Moab on the railroad. Riding the Iron Horse was not a Carnival Cruise. And once the railroad dumped a person off in the desert oasis of Thompson Springs, there were few facilities and very limited travel options. The Thompson to Moab stage was an open-windowed, horse-drawn carriage that took ten to twelve hours of dusty, bone-tiring jostling about to travel the thirty-five miles to town. It is not surprising that tourists didn't visit the area in any numbers until the era of modern roads, soft rubber tires, and air-conditioned automobiles.

By the 1930s, automobiles were common, and the Moab Lion's Club began the first organized efforts to attract tourists to the area. The club also sought an expansion of Arches National Monument, which at the time included only forty-five hundred acres. The Moab newspaper also took an active part in promoting the area. The promise of tourism was seen as a way to supplement a sagging rural economy.

But tourism remained very limited through the 1940s and '50s. Most roads were dirt, and there were few facilities for tourists. Traveling the backcountry was uncomfortable and carried a high degree of risk. In the early 1950s, a large sign near Blanding at the turnoff to Natural Bridges National Monument summed things up pretty well. The sign said:

Drive carefully. This road is safe when dry and when driven at reasonable speeds not to exceed 25 miles pr. hour. Carry ample water and check gas and oil. Use lower gear on steep grades. Reduce to low or second gear before driving through sand. Do not stop in sand. Sound horn on curves and dugways. Do not stop in washes. Stop only on hard ground. Gas, meals, lodging available at Hite and Hanksville [approximately 80 and 125 miles down the road].

It was an era before cell phones, CB radios, GPS technology, OnStar road assistance, automotive air-conditioning, and friendly BLM and National Park Service employees on the back roads. It took a special kind of tourist to do summer vacations in southern Utah in those days—and not many people did.

Moab's Slickrock Bike Trail—twelve miles of scenic splendor
(author photo)

It was the late 1960s before Moab was discovered by a new generation of Americans with big shiny cars, travel trailers, leisure time, and money to spend. Several factors contributed to the increased interest: better roads and accommodations, a more mobile and affluent society, the creation of nearby Canyonlands National Park and Lake Powell with the resulting national publicity, the expansion of Arches National Monument into a national park, the popularity of movies made in the area, the writings of people like Edward Abbey, and a new national awareness of ecology and conservationism coupled with a longing to visit "wilderness" places.

Grand County and the City of Moab also did much to promote the area. The decades from the 1960s through the 1990s saw the creation of dozens of annual events, competitions, festivals, commemorations, races, contests, and promotions designed to bring tourists to the area. Those activities continue through today. A check of Moab Web sites will offer a calendar of events.

Moab's tourist activities are many and varied. Mountain biking is a major focus, but four-wheel drive, motorcycle, and ATV enthusiasts also find plenty to do. The annual spring Jeep Safari brings thousands of people into town for a week of backcountry adventure and amazing demonstrations of high-risk rock crawling by daredevils with expensive, custom-made rigs. The river, too, has become a playground, with dozens of opportunities for boating and rafting.

Hundreds of entrepreneurs have gotten in on the act in the past thirty years, offering everything from snowcones to jeep tours and art exhibits to belly dancers. With a little time and money, visitors can find a plethora of things to see and do. Moab is a famous tourist town now, and service industry jobs have largely replaced the old farming, ranching, and mining jobs. Buildings that once housed mine supply companies now sport restaurants, trading posts, bookstores, and bike shops.

In fact, Moab has become famous as "the" place for mountain biking in the United States. The climate is perfect, and dozens of roads and trails offer unlimited possibilities. People come from all over the world to mountain bike in Moab. The most famous venue is the Slickrock Trail, a twelve-mile circuit just a few miles east of town that runs through some of the most spectacular scenery in America.

Moab has finally been discovered. Today she is one of the premier tourist destinations in the United States. And more important for many of the town's residents, not all of Moab's high school graduates have to leave the area to make a living.

Rocks That Might Kill You and Dirt That's Alive

Slickrock is a term used to describe outcroppings of smooth, weathered sandstone. There are thousands of acres of the stuff around Moab. Slickrock has a surface like concrete that is great for biking and jeeping, but it can be dangerous to hikers. It's easy to lose your footing, and slickrock sheds water instantly. A person doesn't want to be in the bottom of a wash or a narrow slot canyon when the weather forecast or the sky warns of rain. Large areas of slickrock can cause a flash flood in minutes, and you don't have to be in the storm to find yourself caught in a flash flood. A storm ten miles away can send a wall of water at you like a freight train.

Slickrock got its name from cowboys—not because of the water hazard it presents, but because it is dangerous to travel on when your horse is wearing iron shoes. Horses have a tendency to slip and fall when crossing slickrock, especially at high speeds. The danger is compounded when the sandstone is wet. More than a few old range cows learned to head for the slickrock when the cowboys came to rope and brand. Any cowboy with good sense wouldn't run a horse on slickrock, and sneaky old cows had a chance to escape—at least for awhile.

But according to park rangers, one of the greatest sins against nature is to step on something called cryptobiotic soils. Cryptobiotic soils are alive and have a crust of living organisms similar to moss or lichens. Park rangers are on a first name basis with the organisms, which they call Cryptos (krip-tose). Cryptos form a thin, lumpy black crust on the surface of the ground that is found on soils all over the arid West. Cryptos are said to help the soil by sealing in moisture, helping to prevent erosion, and providing stable conditions for the germination of seeds.

So when hiking and biking in the Land of Moab, be cautious of slickrock hazards and try not to trample the black-crusted dirt. Remember, Mother Nature, park rangers, and the ghost of Edward Abbey are watching.

The Long Shadow of
Edward Abbey

his is the most beautiful place on earth." So begins *Desert Solitaire* and Edward Abbey's journey into fame, fortune, and the pages of history. His book is a collection of essays, diary entries, and musings about Arches National Monument (not a park in those days) and the red deserts around Moab in the late 1950s.

Like many visitors to Moab, Abbey was an easterner, bred and born in Pennsylvania, a land of forests, flowing water, grass, and rain. He came west as an employee of the National Park Service and found his heart, voice, and mission among the sandstone spires and desert vistas of the Land of Moab. For three seasons he worked as a ranger at Arches, in a time when few people knew what was there and hardly anyone ever visited. Abbey had "the most beautiful place on earth" all to himself for days on end, and the experience changed him forever.

His *Desert Solitaire: A Season in the Wilderness* was first published in 1968, ten years after his wilderness awakening. It has become a literary classic and a favorite of environmentalists, venerated for the power of the prose, the heartfelt sentiments expressed, and the imagination it inspires. The book is truly a work of art.

Desert Solitaire propelled Abbey to the forefront of the environmental movement of the 1970s and '80s, and it helped to make Arches one of the best known of the national parks. With *Desert*

Solitaire and several other books that followed—twenty-one in all—Abbey found himself to be the voice and champion of everything "Green," an odd caricature for a man who loved red deserts and raw sandstone. His tales of wilderness, solitude, and paradise lost inspired a whole generation of backpackers and wilderness advocates.

Abbey's passionately penned sentiments became the gospel of environmentalism. He is often cited, and many of his disciples quote chapter and verse. He became the Oracle and High Priest of the environmental movement while he lived, and the God of Wilderness following his demise. He was an odd character—it is said that he was buried in a sleeping bag, under a cactus, somewhere in the deserts of Arizona after his death in 1989.

There was a dark side to the man, too. Some of his writings, and especially his 1975 novel *The Monkeywrench Gang*, revealed a penchant for civil disobedience, criminal mischief, and even sabotage in the name of environmentalism. Some have called him an anarchist. *The Monkeywrench Gang* became a textbook and "monkeywrenching" the battle cry for those who call themselves "eco-warriors," the true believers, activists, and soldiers of Mother Earth. His words and works inspired the founding of such organizations as Earth First!, even though Abbey was never officially a member.

Like Charlie Steen, the Uranium King, Ed Abbey helped to put Moab on the map. His writings have inspired untold thousands to venture to Moab to see and feel and do the things he talks about in his books. And yet Abbey hated tourists—the flock the National Park Service hired him to shepherd, and the people most apt to buy his books. He hated tourism, roads, cars, signs, fast food joints, and rules—all of the things his books helped to promote. He surely struggled with the irony of it to the end of his life.

Steen and Abbey were contemporaries who lived in and around Moab at the same time—they might have known each other. They are

Moab's most famous adopted sons, alike in the heavy imprints they left on the community, yet opposites in every way—Steen was the industrialist and Abbey the environmentalist-poet-turned-anarchist.

And yet, in the Land of Moab, Steen is only remembered, while Abbey is worshipped by the very people he hated. Thousands come every year to reverence at his altar, the high desert ridge of Arches National Park. Some who have read his books retrace his steps while searching, often in vain, for the deep feelings of his poet's heart expressed on his pages. Others, more pragmatic, pay homage to his memory by simply buying or re-reading his books. Some of his eco-warriors make sacrifice by sprinkling an offering of good whiskey upon the sand. He would have liked that.

Poet, prophet, Renaissance man, or rogue? He was all of those things and more. One thing is for sure—his memory and his books will be with us for a long, long time to come. Even in death, his shadow stretches far across the desert vistas that he loved.

One Hundred Years
on the Sandrock Trail

* * *
(· *

O ne of Eastern Utah's first forest rangers published a book
about his adventures. The man was John Riis, and his book
is called *Ranger Tales* (Dietz Press, 1937). In his book, Riis
called the road from Crescent Junction through Moab to Monticello
the Sandrock Trail. He first visited the area in 1907 and recorded the
following impressions, as reprinted in *Look to the Mountains* by
Charles S. Peterson (Brigham Young University Press, 1975):

> . . . [Monticello] lies at the end of the Sandrock trail a hun-
> dred dusty miles below the glittering tracks of the Denver and
> Rio Grande [railroad]. Southward you ride, crossing the
> Grand River where sleepy Moab nestles deep between the red
> cliffs, still south over the sun scorched miles of dry valley, then
> up the long pull between the pinyons and the cedars till you
> climb out on the plateaus and to Monticello. . . .

> Moab nestles between red sandstone cliffs at the foot of the
> long valley where the brown waters of the Grand River
> emerge for a bit from a rocky gorge only to disappear again
> into an even narrower gorge that in the end becomes the
> Grand Canyon. In the early days of the west the little

Mormon settlement with the biblical name was just another stopping-off point on the Sandrock trail used by train robbers and other fugitives from the scant laws of the west. The country was almost inaccessible and it was a bold sheriff who would follow the Sandrock trail in search of his man.

One hundred years later, in 2007, the Sandrock Trail is Highway 191. The country has changed a great deal in a hundred years.

Southward you ride from busy Interstate 70, the black arrow of asphalt aimed at red hills in the distance. The road is crowded. Cars, campers, trailers, jeeps, trucks towing boats, little cars with bicycles clinging to racks fore and aft, tour buses, and gypsy vans, all hurry toward Moab. It is an impatient migration. Vacation minutes are quickly ticking by. Go is the byword—everyone straining to get there soon, to see, to do, and to have lots of fun. The whine of speeding traffic echoes from distant ledges, then sprinkles down softly on fields of sage and sand.

Past Canyonlands Airport and Arches View Campground, past the road to Dead Horse Point, down the chute of Moab Canyon, then past the gateway to Arches and across the river bridge the road races. Follow the highway into Moab, where a clutter of signs scream for your attention. Stop here, buy this, do that. Explore, experience, enjoy. Eat, drink, sleep. Tour, float, fly. Join, do, go—a feast of possibilities. Tourists fill the sidewalks, crosswalks, storefronts, and service stations. Everyone in a hurry. Everyone having fun.

South of town the dark ribbon of asphalt continues, still in a hurry, still reaching impatiently toward the distant Blue Mountains. Over hill and dell it wanders, through twists and turns of canyons, over bridges, washes, and waves of sand. Past Hole-in-the-Rock, where sacred red ledges bear garish painted signs and the road is scarred with the skid marks of split-second decisions made to stop and see the sights. Past Wilson Arch, Lisbon Valley, the road to Canyonlands and Church Rock. Onward, onward, the Sandrock Trail streaks toward Monticello, Blanding, Cortez, and Albuquerque. Distant sparkles of sun-touched auto glass move silently across far landscapes, then fade in the desert haze and disappear.

Select Bibliography

Blue Mountain Shadows: The Magazine of San Juan County History.
Blanding, Utah. Various issues.

Canyon Legacy: Journal of the Dan O'Laurie Canyon Country Museum. Moab, Utah. Various issues.

Firmage, Richard A., *A History of Grand County.* Utah State Historical Society. Salt Lake City, 1996.

Geary, Edward A., *A History of Emery County.* Utah State Historical Society. Salt Lake City, 1996.

McPherson, Robert S., *A History of San Juan County.* Utah State Historical Society. Salt Lake City, 1995.

Moab Happenings: Southeast Utah's Event Magazine.

Peterson, Charles S., *Look to the Mountains: Southeast Utah and the LaSal National Forest.* Brigham Young University Press. Provo, Utah, 1975.

Tanner, Fawn McConkie, *The Far Country.* Olympus Publishing Co. Salt Lake City, 1976.

Taylor, Sam, Selected newspaper columns published in Moab's *Times Independent* newspaper.

Watt, Ronald G., *A History of Carbon County.* Utah State Historical Society. Salt Lake City, 1997.

About the Author

TOM MCCOURT IS A NATIVE SON of the deserts and canyons of eastern Utah. He has been a cowboy, a coalminer, a social worker, a freelance writer, and a tour guide. Tom has a degree in Anthropology from the University of Utah and served as an Officer and a Gentleman in the U.S. Army. He and his wife Jeannie make their home in rural Carbon County, Utah.